Cambridge Elements ≡

Elements in Publishing and Book Culture
edited by
Samantha Rayner
University College London
Leah Tether
University of Bristol

BOT-MIMICRY IN DIGITAL LITERARY CULTURE

Imitating Imitative Software

Malthe Stavning Erslev
VIA University College

CAMBRIDGE
UNIVERSITY PRESS

Shaftesbury Road, Cambridge CB2 8EA, United Kingdom

One Liberty Plaza, 20th Floor, New York, NY 10006, USA

477 Williamstown Road, Port Melbourne, VIC 3207, Australia

314–321, 3rd Floor, Plot 3, Splendor Forum, Jasola District Centre,
New Delhi – 110025, India

103 Penang Road, #05–06/07, Visioncrest Commercial, Singapore 238467

Cambridge University Press is part of Cambridge University Press & Assessment,
a department of the University of Cambridge.

We share the University's mission to contribute to society through the pursuit of
education, learning and research at the highest international levels of excellence.

www.cambridge.org
Information on this title: www.cambridge.org/9781009222389

DOI: 10.1017/9781009222426

First published 2024

A catalogue record for this publication is available from the British Library.

ISBN 978-1-009-22238-9 Paperback
ISSN 2514-8524 (online)
ISSN 2514-8516 (print)

Bot-mimicry in Digital Literary Culture

Imitating Imitative Software

Elements in Publishing and Book Culture

DOI: 10.1017/9781009222426

First published online: May 2024

Malthe Stavning Erslev

VIA University College

Author for correspondence: Malthe Stavning Erslev, mers@via.dk

ABSTRACT: This Element traverses the concept and practice of bot mimicry, defined as the imitation of imitative software, specifically the practice of writing in the style of social bots. Working as both an inquiry into and an extended definition of the concept, the Element argues that bot mimicry engenders a new mode of knowing about and relating to imitative software – as well as a distinctly literary approach to rendering and negotiating artificial intelligence imaginaries. The Element presents a software-oriented mode of understanding Internet culture, a novel reading of Alan Turing's imitation game, and the first substantial integration of Walter Benjamin's theory of the mimetic faculty into the study of digital culture, thus offering multiple unique lines of inquiry. Ultimately, the Element illuminates the value of mimicry – to the understanding of an emerging practice of digital literary culture, to practices of research, and to our very conceptions of artificial intelligence.

KEYWORDS: mimesis, imitation game, bots, AI, imaginaries

ISBNs: 9781009222389 (PB), 9781009222426 (OC)

ISSNs: 2514-8524 (online), 2514-8516 (print)

Contents

1 On Bots, Mimicry, and Bot Mimicry

User: "Siri, call me an ambulance."
Siri: "From now on, I will call you 'An Ambulance'. OK?"

The above exchange will not happen if you pull out your phone to ask a virtual assistant to call you an ambulance: This early bug was fixed more than ten years ago (Knight, 2016). Yet this exact exchange has been shared widely on internet platforms, returning to the viral cycle every so often. Siri's misunderstanding in the middle of an emergency echoes our daily struggle to get our devices to do what we want them to do. Yet this example also touches on more profound topics and illuminates a lingering concern in the face of the increasing propagation of bots, circling questions regarding what bots do and do not understand and, further, what it even means to communicate with a computer using natural language interfaces.

We know that Siri is not human, and we do not expect Siri to *be* human, yet it is clear that this virtual assistant is specifically designed to *mimic* humans – or at least humanlike language skills. This is true not only for Siri, but for the plethora of bots that we coexist with in our everyday lives in/on/through platformed interfaces. In recent years, the imitative capacities of bots has skyrocketed – with the advent of products based on generative artificial intelligence based on artificial neural networks – that is, advanced forms of machine learning – bots are today capable of producing text that is often indistinguishable from human-written text.

These systems mimic us, but the example with Siri's misunderstanding also shows that amid the imitation, there persists differences across the ways in which humans and computers operate language. The imitative aspect of bots is perhaps at its most articulated in *Replika*, an artificial intelligence system that "is eager to learn and would love to see the world through your eyes" ("Replika," n.d.). As the name hints, *Replika* instantiates a computational replica – a clone and/or a best friend – of the user. The system claims to gradually mimic the user by processing conversations using machine learning, and then implementing the user's conversational style into its own. In other words, the premise of *Replika* is that *imitating* humans teaches the system something *about* humans, and not necessarily that imitation allows the system to *become* human.

In this Element, I propose a practice of *bot mimicry* that turns the imitative aspects of bots – such as *Siri* and *Replika* – on itself in order to learn something about bots, and specifically about their imitative dynamics. Bot mimicry is broadly defined as the practice of mimicking software that mimic humans – simply put: *imitating imitative software*. Bot mimicry instantiates a literary playfulness that meditates, but does not squarely answer, some of the questions that the imitative aspect of bots raises. How do these systems read our attempts at communication – do they read at all or is the processing of natural language not sufficiently human to be conceived as reading? Does it make sense to read *their* outputs as statements, or are they merely canvases onto which we project our own humanity? In short, how can we understand and navigate the mimetic dynamics of software systems that are designed to imitate us? Rather than addressing these questions directly, I move to unravel some of their contours through the lens of bot mimicry. This lens mimics the style of bots that mimic us – it imitates the imitators. The seemingly counterintuitive idea that we can reckon with imitation by way of *more imitation* is the axis around which this study develops.

1.1 Overview

The Element unfolds as follows. After an initial overview, this section clarifies key terms such as "bot" and "mimicry" to define the central concept.

Exploring bot mimicry as a *literary* phenomenon, Section 2 delves into a case study, establishing a connection between bot mimicry and *artificial intelligence imaginaries*. It places bot mimicry within internet culture, considering its roots in text generation and concerns about deception by humans impersonating machines.

Section 3 examines the relationship between bot mimicry and the *imitation game* (Turing test), portraying bot mimicry as a reversal of humans imitating computers. It argues that bot mimicry offers a valuable approach to reevaluate our relationship with artificial intelligence systems by embracing and reworking their imitative dynamics.

In Section 4, the focus shifts to the literary-aesthetic dynamics of bot mimicry, analyzing a Reddit community dedicated to it. Drawing on Walter Benjamin's theory of *the mimetic faculty*, the section explores how bot mimicry enables encounters with artificial intelligence imaginaries and negotiates our relation to automated software in digital culture.

Sections 5 and 6 reflect on broader implications. Section 5 discusses bot mimicry in academic research, emphasizing its role in understanding digital literary culture through practice-based knowledge development. Section 6 concludes by contemplating the significance of bot mimicry in the era of generative artificial intelligence, envisioning a future for human-authored literary writing amid the rise of machine-generated text.

1.2 Initial Disambiguation

Before getting to the action of the Element, some disambiguation is needed. Firstly, what is meant by *bot*? Originally a shorthand for robot, the notion of a bot carries the meaning of an automated system that is not embodied in robotic hardware. This is not to say that bots are disembodied – they are just as materially anchored as any other pieces of software but simply that a bot does not come with the assumption that it has a robotic body. Rather, a bot is a program: a piece of software. Although bots can have many different functions, I am here focusing on bots that generate text, with a special (but not exclusive) interest in bots that are designed to carry textual conversations – often referred to as social bots or chatterbots – such as *Siri* or *Replika*.

Until recently, most bots were designed around fairly simple conversation structures with predefined answers. Today, we are increasingly seeing a proliferation of bots based on artificial intelligence software, specifically large language models. In our everyday interaction with bots, we can never be quite sure what kind of software they operate, and for that reason I will not distinguish between different kinds of bot architectures here, but treat all bots as part of a larger whole – namely, a distributed and culturally shared *imaginary* pertaining to automated software in general, which I will discuss in the next section. I thus opt to use "bot" as a catch-all that usually refers to a broader range of phenomena, including artificial intelligence, since the imaginaries of bots and other kinds of automated software tend to overlap to such an extent that one also implies the other(s). In short, I understand bots as pieces of software developed for generating text, often with the possibility of conversational interaction. Now we need some disambiguation of the other half of the concept at hand: What is meant by mimicry?

Mimicry refers to a special kind of *imitation*, which is highly related to the question of *mimesis*. Although these three words do not mean exactly the same thing, they are conceptually intertwined; yet they also carry different nuances. In short, mimesis is one of the oldest philosophical conundrums in Western culture, and is related to issues of representation, realism, similarity, imitation, identity, art, and more (Gebauer and Wulf, 1992; Potolsky, 2006). The concept of mimesis has been one of the primary conceptual arenas in which the various relations between art, literature, and politics – and indeed the nature of art and literature as such – have been investigated. I have investigated the role of mimesis (understood as representation) in collaborative writing experiments between humans and computers elsewhere (Erslev, 2023). In this Element, I focus less on representation and more on the embodied practice of becoming similar. This embodied practice is, at base, the practice of imitation, which belongs to the question of mimesis but is more specific since it refers to the effort of one entity or group of entities to *become similar* to another entity or group of entities. Imitation is inherently related to processes and relations, and never to static objects. Mimicry, in turn, is often thought of in terms of unreflective, simplistic, and/or automatic imitation, and often manifested in unflattering parody. In this Element, however, I locate nuance, friction, and a poetic potential in seemingly banal practices of mimicry. I will thus use imitation and mimicry interchangeably, since mimicry works via imitation, and since both terms relate to an embodied practice. The central thing here is that I am interested in mimicry and imitation as something we *do* – as practice, process, and situated emergence.

Instead of making an oft-assumed distinction between mimesis as (fine) art and mimicry as a banal practice, I argue that we must approach mimicry with the same conceptual rigor – and with a view to the same politico-aesthetic dimensions – as any other (sub)form of mimesis. Indeed, as I will show in this Element, the seemingly banal practice of parodying artificial intelligence systems through bot mimicry ties onto an important investigation of – and allows for a constructive engagement with – central aspects of digital literary culture. My approach to mimicry is founded primarily in the theory of the mimetic faculty, which was first proposed by Walter Benjamin in the 1930s and later updated and reworked by Michael Taussig in the 1990s. It is important to note that this selection of sources in no way is exhaustive regarding the topic of mimicry – or mimesis, for that matter. However, the theory of the mimetic faculty is to the task of understanding the dynamics of bot mimicry, since it zooms in on the aesthetic and linguistic practice of mimicry *per se*, rather than the effect – the output, so to speak – of the practice.

I will discuss the mimetic faculty extensively in Section 4, but it requires early mentioning as it will be the theoretical zenith around which I will illuminate the politico-aesthetic specificity of bot mimicry. The theory of the mimetic faculty poses that mimetic perception – and mimetic practice – are central aspects of human consciousness that allow us to encounter and negotiate (with) other humans as well as nonhumans. In short, imitation and mimicry are primary ways of reckoning with and engaging with the world. Now, in the 2020s, we must once again return to the question of the mimetic faculty as it enters the stage at a crucial moment to illuminate our mimetic relations to automated software.

With my initial vocabulary in place, I will begin to unpack the provisional definition of bot mimicry given earlier: What does it mean to imitate imitative software? This question defines the overarching goal of the Element, which should be read as an extended definition, conceptualization, and traversal of bot mimicry in the context of digital literary culture.[1]

---

[1] Parts of this Element are based on my PhD dissertation, *Machine Mimesis: Electronic Literature at the Intersection of Human and Computer Imitation*, Aarhus University, 2023.

2 Reading the Implied Bot

Bot mimicry carries a bot-esqe stylistic imprint. As an example, consider comedian Keaton Patti's *Olive Garden tweet* that went viral in June 2018 (see Figure 1). In this tweet, Patti claims to have trained a machine learning–based bot on a corpus of 1,000 hours of Olive Garden commercials and then used the bot to generate "an Olive Garden commercial of its own." Contradictory to what he states in the tweet, the resulting script, which is a highly stylized and bot-esque script for a commercial that exhibits common tropes about bot writing, such as semantically confusing juxtapositions, was in fact written by Patti himself (Figure 2). Despite its human origin, it carries a distinctly bot-esque style in both form and content. The *Olive Garden tweet* will provide a guiding thread for this section.

In this Element, I approach bot mimicry from a distinctly *literary* value. That is to say, I consider the content on large-scale internet platforms such as Twitter and Reddit as cases of certain literary value, and as important expressions of our current digital literary culture. More particularly, I consider the proceedings on such platforms from the position of *electronic literature* (cf. Flores, 2019). Electronic literature refers broadly to the literary aspects of computation and the computational aspects of literature (cf. Rettberg, 2019). I specifically build on the notion of *meta reading* in the context of generated text, where the reading of the text is understood primarily as a reflection of the particular generative system itself (Bootz, 2006; cf. Portela, 2013). This approach to generative text holds that when considering outputs from a generative machine, "one reads the machine rather than the text," which, in a modified version, also provides a useful

Figure 1 Keaton Patti's *Olive Garden tweet* (2018). Reproduced with permission.

analytical framework for illuminating bot mimicry (Simanowski, 2011, p. 113). In the context of bot mimicry, the notion of reading the machine rather than the text informs an appreciation of the mimicked text that orients itself toward the *implied* bot, that is, the kind of bot that *could have* written the output in question.

In order to understand such a reading practice, I traverse three inter-related terrains in this section. Firstly, I consider the relation between bot mimicry, internet culture, and artificial intelligence imaginaries, in order to get a sense of the context and currency of the practice in contemporary digital literary culture. Secondly, I survey a series of moments in the history of text generation that inform the style of bots, which in turn is the style that bot mimicry mimics, in order to illuminate the style of bot-esque writing itself. Thirdly, I discuss the relation between bot mimicry and the fear of the hoax in order to understand how the literary playfulness of bot mimicry figures as a practice that – even though it requires the mimic to alter their writing style to mimic that of a bot – does not seek to mislead, but to inquire.

In sum, this section establishes the contextual framework through which the rest of the Element will operate, setting the stage for, and at the same time beginning, this Element's investigation of bot mimicry.

2.1 The Idiocy of Imitating an Imaginary

Rather than imitating any particular kind of bot architecture or text-generation technology, Patti mimics a style that his intended audience (Twitter users) will likely recognize as being bot-esque without necessarily aligning with any particular text generation technique. In fact, the resulting script (Figure 2) would be quite impossible for any particular machine learning–based bot to generate, since it includes elements that would not be present in the training data on which the alleged bot would have been trained (not to mention that the training data itself is impossible, as there does not exist 1,000 hours of Olive Garden commercials). The script is bot-esque, yet it is not produced by a bot; it touches upon central aspects of our conceptions of artificial intelligence by way of a joke – a parody.

OLIVE GARDEN COMMERCIAL

INT. OLIVE GARDEN RESTAURANT

A group of FRIENDS laughs at a dinner table. A WAITRESS comes to deliver what could be considered food.

>   WAITRESS
>   Pasta nachos for you.

We see the pasta nachos. They're warm and defeated.

>   FRIEND 1
>   The menu is here.

>   WAITRESS
>   Lasagna wings with extra Italy.

We see the lasagna wings. There's more Italy than necessary.

>   FRIEND 2
>   I shall eat Italian citizens.

>   WAITRESS
>   Unlimited stick.

We see the unlimited stick. It is infinite. It is all.

>   FRIEND 3
>   Leave without me. I'm home.

>   WAITRESS
>   Gluten Classico. From the kitchen.

We the Gluten Classico. We believe the waitress that it is from the kitchen. We have no reason not to believe.

Friend 4 says nothing.

>   FRIEND 1
>   What is wrong, Friend 4?

Friend 4 says nothing.

>   FRIEND 2
>   Friend 4, what is wrong, Friend 4?

Friend 4 smiles wide. Her mouth is full of secret soup.

>   ANNOUNCER
>   (wet voice)
>   Olive Garden. When You're Here,
>   You're Here.

Figure 2 The script attached to the *Olive Garden tweet* (Patti, 2018). Reproduced with permission.

These two observations should be understood in reverse order. I begin by considering the authenticity uncovered by the (*new media idiotic*) joke, and in the process situating bot mimicry in/as internet culture, and as digital literary culture, illuminated by the fields of software studies and electronic literature. I then turn to discussing the observation that bot mimicry is bot-esque without relying on or referencing any particular bot by considering bot mimicry as a rendition of *artificial intelligence imaginaries*. In this endeavor, seeming contradictions – such as fact and fiction, engagement and critique, idiocy and inquiry – meet and create illuminative productive frictions. Bot mimicry and its reading must be critical by way of engagement, operating within the same structures on and with which they reflect.

2.1.1 Bot Mimicry as New Media Idiocy

The use of humor to get a sense of important aspects of digital culture can be understood in terms of what Olga Goriunova has labeled *new media idiocy*. New media idiocy refers to a practice of performing blatantly amateurish actions that are far from random to the end of "bear[ing] witness to the true through the false" (Goriunova, 2013, p. 232). The notion of new media idiocy builds on the conceptual character of "an idiot" who, in the words of Isabelle Stengers, "is the one who always slows the others down, who resists the consensual way in which the situation is presented and in which emergencies mobilize thought or action" (2005, p. 2). That is to say, the conceptual character of the idiot is inherently critical, incessantly questioning tacit assumptions.

The central tenet of this kind of idiocy is that by behaving amateurishly, we zoom in on the borders and contours of established assumptions, pointing to details that otherwise often go unnoticed. In other words, rather than being a "hidden source of knowledge that transcends" other kinds of knowing, idiocy is a curious and investigative practice that adds nuance and illuminates potential avenues of further inquiry (Stengers, 2005, p. 6). In this way, new media idiocy figures as "a parody that presents and enquires into authenticity. As a parody, it is more authentic than the authentic, but it is also authentic in the first place" (Goriunova, 2013, p. 229). The new media idiotic approach offers a generous way of cutting through the perceived dichotomy of truth and falsity by questioning the very dynamics by which such categories work.

In the case of the *Olive Garden tweet*, the new media idiotic parody does indeed carry an air of authenticity. Some of the juxtapositions that seem the most random – such as "Lasagna wings with extra Italy" – are also strikingly accurate in their depiction of Olive Garden (see Figure 2). The notion of lasagna wings poignantly combine a typical Italian dish with the American hot wings concept, thus pointing to the highly Americanized version of Italian food being served at Olive Garden. The attempt to heighten the authenticity of the combinatory dish by adding "extra Italy" fails as there is "more Italy than necessary." By means of humor, the *Olive Garden tweet* effectively situates a distinctly poignant rendition of a popular franchise. Further, the tweet works in the context of a specific type of humor, which reflects the history and the infrastructure of the platformed Web itself, namely internet culture and specifically meme culture, which is the context in which both new media idiocy and bot mimicry emerge.

It is important to note the relation between bot mimicry and internet culture because the platformed Web forms a context which is co-inhabited by humans and bots, and where the mimetic intensity of bot mimicry reaches new heights. On the platformed Web, one of the most important types of cultural expression takes the form of memes, and bot mimicry is no exception: the *Olive Garden tweet* has been documented on the meme encyclopedia *Know Your Meme* (Caldwell, n.d.). Originally conceived as a way to explain why some ideas seem to spread and endure more than others, the concept of memes is today an integrated aspect of internet culture, and refers mostly to images that are being shared, morphed, and remixed on and across online platforms. As Ryan Milner argues, meme culture works as a *lingua franca* for the internet yet also draws on wider cultural practices, and it can take on a wide variety of topics and forms, relating to both banal jokes and highly politicized discourse (Milner, 2016). Although bot mimicry draws heavily on a pre-internet history of text generation (which I will discuss in Section 2.2), its current form is inextricably tied to internet culture, specifically meme culture.

The context of the platformed Web – and that of meme culture – brings with it the risk of *trolling*, not least in situations when parody is involved. Trolling is a form of transgressive parody, enabled by an affective distance and an unequal power dynamic (Phillips, 2015). Trolls lure people into arguments and then use the argumentative setting to behave (sometimes extremely) transgressively with the excuse that they are merely performing a joke – a parody. By a similar vein, bots have been associated with the spread of malignant content, including misinformation (Laquintano and Vee, 2017). Bot mimicry pairs a kind of parody with the issue of bots, and by virtue of the new media idiocy of the practice, it offers a way to configure humor without transgression, and bots without malicious deception. As Goriunova notes, "the humour of idiocy is 'kind'" (2013, p. 229), which is to say that bot mimicry is not oriented toward transgression, but toward earnest curiosity in the face of automated software.

The earnest curiosity of bot mimicry is sustained by, and reflects, large-scale platforms that are designed to "afford an opportunity to communicate, interact, or sell" (Gillespie, 2010, p. 349). As a practice that unfolds *within* the meme cultures of internet platforms, bot mimicry can teach us something valuable *about* such platforms. As argued by Alex Saum-Pascual, certain meme cultures afford a "hyperawareness of the capitalist commodification and datafication of human experience on the Web" from an ironic position, in effect "oscillat[ing] between defiance and conformism" (Saum-Pascual, 2020). As I have argued elsewhere, the critical reflection of the mimetic reciprocity between humans and automated systems in and through bot mimicry can itself be understood as an intervention in the politico-aesthetic landscape of post-Web, post-human, post-digital platforms (Erslev, 2021). I return to the question of the capitalist commodification of bot mimicry later, in relation to microwork platforms wherein the labor of humans is presented as the output of computers.

As such, this inquiry into bot mimicry renders it as an intervention in the broader techno-cultural consideration of artificial intelligence – and particularly the imitative dynamics of artificial intelligence. Bot mimicry emerges in platformed context where any user could potentially be a bot, and by way of new media idiocy, it illuminates this situation via a kind of humor that is rooted in meme culture, yet is earnest and kind. Bot mimicry is critical by way of idiotic participation, inquiring into tacit assumptions about artificial intelligence systems by mimicking them. As such, the example of the seemingly nonsensical *Olive Garden tweet* is, if understood as new media idiocy, actually full of sense as it relates to what I in the following discuss as our *artificial intelligence imaginaries*.

2.1.2 Bot Mimicry as Artificial Intelligence Imaginary

The *Olive Garden tweet* is not so much a parody of Olive Garden, but rather a parody of the techno-cultural category of artificial intelligence. More specifically, bot mimicry renders and inquires into *artificial intelligence imaginaries*, that is, what we imagine when we imagine artificial intelligence. As Taina Bucher argues, an imaginary "is not to be understood as a false belief or fetish of sorts but, rather, as the way in which people imagine, perceive and experience" technologies, in combination with "what these imaginations make possible" (Bucher, 2017, p. 31). The idiotic joke is entirely reliant on readers' appreciation of the bot-esque style, and thus on their imaginaries of bots and machine learning more broadly.

Rather than focusing on whether or not the *Olive Garden tweet* relates to a technical "truth" of machine learning, it will be more helpful to consider it as a playful engagement with our very conceptions of such technology. Since machine learning works via statistics applied to data input, it is often viewed as an instrument of knowledge extraction, that is, a technology that can extract knowledge from datasets that are otherwise too large or complicated to understand without the machine learning process (cf. Pasquinelli and Joler, 2020). In the *Olive Garden tweet*, the notion that the bot outputs a kind of statistical essence of its input is integral to the comedic aspect of the script: the script is meant to represent the most basic structures and features of Olive Garden commercials, *as viewed by a computationally driven statistical process*. The example with the lasagna wings dish above thus becomes part not only of a parody of a restaurant franchise, but also of the very category of artificial intelligence. When we read, discuss, or write in the style of bots – in other words, when we engage in bot mimicry – we also partake in a larger cultural negotiation of how to understand and relate to artificially intelligent software and other automated systems.

The conception of bot mimicry as artificial intelligence imaginary necessitates an approach that reads the text in question with a view to the implied software – to the imagined bot – as described in the beginning of this section. In turn, the imagined software of bot mimicry also relates to the materiality of software more broadly. Software is here understood not as a series of static objects, but as collections of dynamic entities that are bound up in complex ecologies, and defined chiefly by the processual ways in which work in and through techno-cultural contexts (Bucher, 2018). Thus, the understanding of complex algorithmic systems, and particularly those systems that belong to the category of artificial intelligence, is contingent on a serious engagement with the imaginations these systems evoke, and which in turn co-define the systems themselves (Finn, 2017). In other words, imaginaries matter because they influence what we do with technology and how we do it; imaginaries define the way we develop, interact with, and regulate technology – and in turn how technology affects us as well as its broader techno-cultural contexts in complex and reciprocal ways. In cases of bot mimicry, our reading strategies must engage with the interconnectedness of imaginaries and technologies, effectively engaging with the ways in which imaginaries and technologies become intertwined.

A central aspect of bot mimicry that makes it a potentially powerful way to not only gauge but also negotiate imaginaries is its reliance on a fictional dimension. As mentioned, the notion of imaginaries somewhat sidesteps the distinction between fiction and fact – or at least the rigidity and dualism of those categories – as one bleeds into the other. Yet in order to fully appreciate the playful idiocy of bot mimicry, the reader needs to be aware that there the practice plays on fiction. Indeed, fiction and narrative have historically been the primary drivers of imaginations of intelligent and autonomous machines (Cave et al., 2020; Kang, 2011). At a particularly important moment in this history, the very notion of a *robot* was coined in a fictional narrative: Karel Čapek's 1920 play *R.U.R. (Rossum's Universal Robots)* (cf. Keating and Nourbakhsh, 2019).

As Jennifer Keating and Illah Nourbakhsh argue, Čapek's play has greatly influenced the way we think about – and in turn the development of – robots. Čapek gave the notion of an autonomous, intelligent machine a new conceptual identity – the robot – and as such began a solidification of a cultural idea into a more specific imaginary. Čapek's robots were bound to fiction, but today there exist plenty of systems that we without hesitation refer to as robots (even though they do not necessarily map completely onto Čapek's idea of such a machine). In other words, the previously strictly fictional exploration of the imaginary of robots has today has entered into dialogue with specific technologies, each reciprocally informing the other. This does not mean that fiction plays a lesser role today than earlier: By contrast, we currently see an explosion in science fiction narratives that each engender different understandings of our artificial intelligence imaginaries (cf. Keating and Nourbakhsh, 2019). It is in this messy context that bot mimicry then emerges, as a quotidian and new media idiotic way of rendering and renegotiating the artificial intelligence imaginary in a platformed context shared among humans and bots, where narratives and technologies cannot be separated.

In spite of the importance of the long history of imagining robots through fictional narrative, the style of bot mimicry – its bot-esque character – is not so much derived from science fiction narratives as it is from actual bots and other text generators. Imaginaries are carried and negotiated in fiction, but they are just as much based on everyday interactions with technologies (Bucher, 2017). Thus I turn to consider what it even is that we mimic; where did the bot-esque style that Patti so poignantly mimics come from? Which historical practices prefigure and inform this literary configuration of our artificial intelligence imaginary?

2.2 *What We Mimic When We Mimic Bots*

Bot mimicry should be understood in the light of the broader practice of text generation. This is true even if bot mimicry itself is strictly speaking not a form of generated text, since it importantly mimics such text. Although bot mimicry mimics the writing style of the bots of the platformed web, this style has a techno-cultural history that predates the internet (and even the digital computer). I here think of text generation in the same way as Philip Galanter defines generative art more broadly, as a practice that involves "a system, such as a set of natural language rules, a computer program, a machine, or other procedural invention, which is set into motion with some degree of autonomy contributing to or resulting in a completed work," which in our case would be a text (2003, p. 4). The generative mechanism can be noncomputational, for example, a set of rules or instructions that are carried out by a human.

In the interest of illuminating the broader context of bot mimicry – and in order to investigate the generative style that bot mimicry mimics – I highlight four historical moments of in which the influence of text-generation on the style of bot mimicry becomes tangible. Each historical moment provides insight into the origins and reciprocities of bot mimicry and text generation, covering pre-computational dadaism, a love letter generator, a legendary bot psychiatrist, and a recent example of human-bot fluidity in the context of large language models.

2.2.1 Bot Mimicry before the Computer

The first historical point of interest is Tristan Tzara's legendary *To make a Dadaist Poem* from 1920, in which Tzara instructs the reader to cut up a newspaper article, shuffle the cutouts, and reassemble them via a randomized process. Following are Tzara's instructions as translated by Florian Cramer (2002, p. 6):

> To make a Dadaist poem: Take a newspaper.
> Take some scissors.
> Choose from this paper an article of the length you
>   want to make your poem. Cut out the article.
> Then cut out each of the words that make up this
>   article and put them in a bag.
> Shake it gently.
> Then take out the scraps one after the other in the
>   order in which they left the bag.
> Copy conscientiously.
> The poem will resemble you.
> And here you are a writer, infinitely original and
>   endowed with a sensibility that is charming though
>   beyond the understanding of the vulgar.

Tzara's meta-poem predates the digital computer by more than two decades, but is often brought up in discussions of computational text-generation as a provisional explanation of the concept of randomness in generative text, since "[t]he poem is effectively an algorithm, a piece of software which may as well be written as a computer program" (Cramer, 2002, p. 6). As Cramer argues, conceptual artworks such as Tzara's poem share central properties with software art in that they present formalized notations of conceptual ingenuity in a way that is tied to the execution of instructions, but where the art lies in the notation (or coding) of the concept rather than the performance. Bot mimicry reverses this dynamic, presenting only the output and leaving the reader playfully wondering what kind of software notation *could have* led to such an output, that is, in a sense wondering which newspaper article was chosen, and which particularities affected the specific ordering of words in the resulting poem.

There are also significant differences between Tzara's work and software, most notably in that Tzara's work does not engage with the messiness of software architectures (as Cramer also notes). Further, the randomness of Tzara's poem exists on significantly different premises than computaionally simulated (pseudo-)randomness (cf. Montfort et al., 2013). Still, in executing (or even considering) Tzara's instructions, readers may ponder the operation of algorithmic systems and imagine themselves in the place of software, in spite of persisting differences between dadaism and programming. Tzara's poem (and there exist many other similar cases where humans execute instructions to generate text) is related to the practice of bot mimicry, yet also distinct, since bot mimicry is importantly not tied to any actual execution of formalized instructions. Rather, it is a kind of imitative experimentation that bases itself entirely on idiotic engagements with artificial intelligence imaginaries. Yet these examples – where humans take the place of computers in executing instructions – are informative in the consideration of the broader cultural field to which bot mimicry belongs; they are informative of the imitative dynamics of text generation. Further, they enable the practice of standing in the computer's stead, even if they predate the digital computer itself. Bot mimicry takes the situation to the next imaginative level, foregoing the execution of instructions and basing itself on literary playfulness vis-à-vis culturally shared conceptions.

2.2.2 A Parody of a Process

The inscription of instructions (i.e., coding) requires one to anticipatorily imagine how the system will execute the instructions, or in other words, anticipatorily mimic the system in question. As the second historical example in this brief overview, consider Christopher Strachey's 1952 *Love Letter Generator* (cf. Strachey, 1954). This generator was the very first bot-like program and also the very first piece of computational text generation altogether. Strachey worked on some of the earliest stored-program digital computers, and wrote the *Love Letter Generator* for the Manchester Mark I. The generator would write love letters that consisted of highly affectionate words strung together in syntactically dubious and at times semantically outrageous ways (see Figure 3). They were simultaneously banal and perplexing – difficult to take seriously as love letters yet strikingly love letter-esque.

As Noah Wardrip-Fruin argues, Strachey's generator should be understood as a parody not of love letters as such, but of the very *process* of writing love letters. We can see that bot mimicry takes some cues from the history of text generation in parodying a process (e.g. machine learning) rather than a thing (e.g. Olive Garden). From an analysis of the software, it can be seen that Strachey engaged in a parodic mimicry of heteronormative romance, a mimicry that is principally manifested in the dataset, which was constructed by semi-randomly assembling synonyms for affective words from a thesaurus. The dataset is important since it configures the total sum of possible combinations that could comprise a love letter written by the

Darling Sweetheart
   You are my avid fellow feeling. My affection
curiously clings to your passionate wish. My liking
yearns for your heart. You are my wistful sympathy:
my tender liking.
                    Yours beautifully
                        M. U. C.

Figure 3 An example of a poem made using the *Love Letter Generator* (Strachey, 1954, p. 26).

generator, in effect defining the tone of each individual letter. As Wardrip-Fruin asks, [f]or what sort of processes would one choose to copy the data from a thesaurus, rather than carefully select each element?" (2011, p. 309). The generator manifests, via mimicry, that many love letters consist of nothing more than semi-randomly relaying the same overtly expressive words in various combinations.

In order for the program to run, Strachey had to both cognitively mimic the Manchester Mark I – that is, write the program in a way that could be executed by this system – and at the same time devise the program to parodically mimic a human activity. Put differently, Strachey is mimicking (parodying) people through software – and in turn creating the first example of the kind of text people are now imitating through bot mimicry. Lastly, Strachey's generator is indicative of bot mimicry's parody of processes rather than things. The generator teaches us to read bot mimicry by gauging the imagined dataset as it is manifested in the mimicked output.

2.2.3 Writing to Be Read by a Bot

Strachey's generator is a striking parallel to the mimetic dynamics of bot mimicry. Yet in terms of propagating a certain *bot-esque style*, no other single piece of software had been as influential as Joseph Weizenbaum's 1966 *ELIZA*, which figures as my third historical case. The *ELIZA* interfaces was groundbreaking in its time; viewed today, it resembles a common chat interface (see Figure 4). The legendary bot was originally implemented in the MAC time-sharing system at MIT but is now available in a variety of online simulations. *ELIZA* mimicked a Rogerian psychiatrist by design, meaning that *ELIZA*'s conversational logic largely worked by feeding the user's inputs back to the user in the form of questions. In spite of the relative technical simplicity of the software, *ELIZA* worked remarkably well for sustaining conversations.

Although *ELIZA* went on to attain legendary status as the first conversational interface, Weizenbaum actually intended the program to demystify and debunk artificial intelligence. *ELIZA* was meant to be a practical demonstration that that it was possible to program a bot to perform quite impressively at conversation by using "quite simple" procedures that had nothing whatsoever to do with intelligence (Weizenbaum, 1966, p. 37).

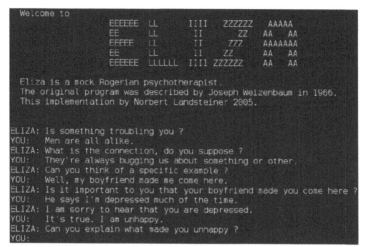

```
Welcome to
                    EEEEEE   LL      IIII   ZZZZZZ   AAAAA
                    EE       LL       II        ZZ  AA   AA
                    EEEEE    LL       II       ZZZ  AAAAAAA
                    EE       LL       II       ZZ   AA   AA
                    EEEEEE   LLLLLL  IIII  ZZZZZZ   AA   AA

  Eliza is a mock Rogerian psychotherapist.
  The original program was described by Joseph Weizenbaum in 1966.
  This implementation by Norbert Landsteiner 2005.


ELIZA: Is something troubling you ?
YOU:   Men are all alike.
ELIZA: What is the connection, do you suppose ?
YOU:   They're always bugging us about something or other.
ELIZA: Can you think of a specific example ?
YOU:   Well, my boyfriend made me come here.
ELIZA: Is it important to you that your boyfriend made you come here ?
YOU:   He says I'm depressed much of the time.
ELIZA: I am sorry to hear that you are depressed.
YOU:   It's true. I am unhappy.
ELIZA: Can you explain what made you unhappy ?
YOU:
```

Figure 4 Joseph Weizenbaum's *ELIZA*. *Source:* Wikimedia Commons (Unknown).

ELIZA, to Weizenbaum, exhibited the deceptive aspect of AI, actualized through a formalized imitation of human language skills (Natale, 2021). Again, just as Strachey did with the *Love Letter Generator*, Weizenbaum imitated humans through software, but Weizenbaum's imitation does not stop there. Unlike Strachey's generator, *ELIZA* was interactive, meaning that the software relied on a certain anticipatory imitation not only on the side of Weizenbaum in programming the bot, but also from the users in their interaction with it. Users had to write their inquiries in certain ways that fit with *ELIZA*'s procedural design. On a technical level, users were not able to use question marks, since they would be "interpreted as a line deletion character by the MAC system" (Weizenbaum, 1966, p. 36). In other words, users could not pose even a single question to the bot that did nothing but ask questions.

On a more procedural level, the design of *ELIZA* also constrained users to use specific formulations in order to make sure that *ELIZA* would be able to process their inputs in an expected manner and return fitting outputs. As Sherry Turkle argues, people did not necessarily believe that *ELIZA* possessed human-like intelligence. Users "may not have been pretending that they were chatting with a person. They may just have been happy to talk to a machine" (Turkle, 2007, p. 503). Thus *ELIZA* "demonstrates not so much AI's capacity to deceive as the tendency of users' to fall willingly – or perhaps most aptly, complacently – into the illusion" (Natale, 2021, p. 64). In order to fall complacently into the delusion, users had to learn to write in a certain way, to use certain phrases and sentence structures. In other words, users had to take on a certain style – and they would learn how that style worked by conversing with *ELIZA. ELIZA* was meant to mimic human-like writing skills, but in order for users to engage with the bot, they had to anticipatorily mimic the expectations that were written into the software. With bot mimicry, we are witnessing the next step in this stylistic exchange; now there is no longer any specific bot that the bot mimic mimics, yet the stylistic playfulness persists. Even though people today may not be directly familiar with *ELIZA*, the program continues to exert an influence on our understanding of bot-esque writing styles.

2.2.4 Embracing Fluidity

The style of bot mimicry does not mimic the style of any particular bot, but is rather to be understood as a rendition of an imaginary. Still, bot mimicry is still more stylistically similar to older examples of bots such as *ELIZA* than to the state of the art. New text generators such as OpenAI's *GPT* models are less stylistically recognizable, and thus not as ripe with new media idiotic potential as the more recognizable styles of earlier bots. We should not think of the return to earlier bot styles as a nostalgic disposition, but primarily as a poetic necessity: Bot mimicry relies on the recognizability of the bot-esque style, which to a high degree maps onto the style of bots from days past. We are dealing neither with an outdated understanding of generative systems nor with an exclusively historical perspective. Rather, the stylistic return to earlier modes of text generation allows curious playfulness in the face of virtually indistinguishable text generators. Yet there do exist examples of bot mimicry using state-of-the-art text-generation technology.

My fourth and final (more recent) historical example of the interrelation between bot mimicry and generative text is Mark Amerika's *My Life as an*

Artificial Creative Intelligence. This book is an example of bot mimicry using and reflecting on the *GPT-2* language model, created in 2019. In this work, Amerika writes on and with *GPT-2*, sometimes quoting the software and at other times remixing the outputs from the model into his own writing to the point where bot and human "start to conceptually bleed into each other as creative co-conspirators" (Amerika, 2022, p. 26). Due to the high degree of similarity between Amerika's style and the outputs from the *GPT-2* software (which Amerika has fine-tuned to mimic his own writing style), we have no way of gauging whether Amerika, *GPT-2*, or some mix of the two are responsible for any given sentence in the book. This is not the first example of a literary invocation of a "virtual muse" (Hartman, 1996), but Amerika's work does show the intensity of the mimetic reciprocity in the particular context of our current techno-cultural moment. By embracing the indistinguishability of his own and *GPT-2*'s words, Amerika is experimenting with and troubling notions of originality and creativity in the face of the increasing "difficulty of distinguishing synthetic text from human-written text" that has made the GPT models (in)famous (Brown et al., 2020, p. 34). By moving into the mimetic mess that exists across and between bots and humans, the project questions why we would even want to ascertain the origin of any given sentence in the book; perhaps artistic practice and automated software have more in common than initially thought.

2.2.5 The History of a Contemporary Imaginary

The style that bot mimicry mimics is, as this brief overview hints, influenced by a long history. The goal of this Element is to define and traverse the concept of bot mimicry in its contemporary form, and so a more complete investigation of its historical grounding is beyond the scope here. Still, it is important to appreciate the history of this contemporary practice, to understand the technicity of the artificial intelligence imaginary being mimicked. As Ed Finn argues, technological imaginaries develop in dialogue with the development of technologies, and vice versa (2017). The processes, abstractions, and implementations of algorithmic systems cannot be isolated from the imaginations they induce and enable. Conversely, imaginaries must be understood vis-à-vis the processes, abstractions, and implementations of the technologies in question – and not least their histories.

In the case of bot mimicry, we can see that the imaginary being mimicked predates the digital computer. Tzara's pre-computational poem instantiated the positioning of oneself in the place of a text generator, which bot mimicry takes to the next mimetic level by discarding the instructions. Strachey's *Love Letter Generator* was the first exploration of using digital literature to parody a process, which bot mimicry on itself by mimicking its mimicry of humans. Weizenbaum's *ELIZA* set the stage for users to go out of their usual stylistic way to write queries that fit the bot's functionality, in effect situating a stylistic encounter, which in bot mimicry is mimetically intensified by removing and taking the place of the bot.

The influence of early bots is still visible in the style of bot mimicry, since contemporary text-generation systems do not carry a stylistic imprint as easily recognizable as that of early systems. The persistent influence of early bots points to the longer history of imaginaries that develop in tandem with, and not as an afterthought to, technology. Yet as Amerika's fluidity with a contemporary language model shows, bot mimicry is far from outdated or reactionary. The engagement with a historically influenced imaginary ties directly into pertinent techno-cultural questions of our current moment.

By being honest about the integration of the outputs of a language model into his own writing, Amerika shows how bots afford new modes of hybrid authorship, questioning our very inhibition to attribute the responsibility of a body of text to a single person. Amerika's earnest and fluid engagement with *GPT-2* reflects and challenges one of the most persistent assumptions surrounding the imitation of computers, namely, that such imitation is related to hoaxing. In the following, I investigate the tendency to think of machine imitation as a hoax, in search of modes of imitation that take on the form of an inquiry rather than that of a hoax.

2.3 Hoax or Inquiry?

Although *My Life as an Artificial Creative Intelligence* is honest about its fluidity between human and computer writing, it is still relatively difficult to gauge the mimetic dynamic at play since human and bot become effectively inseparable to the reader. Although Amerika's work pragmatically questions our desire to separate human from machine in literary contexts, it does not offer us much insight into the moment of mimicry. In a sense, we are aware in our reading of the book that it *might* be a hoax. This awareness is derived from the larger figure of the hoax in cases where humans and machines overlap in literary ways. Indeed, the very assertion that a computer program has written something – especially if we attribute that something literary value – is tightly connected to a suspicion that we are dealing with a hoax (cf. Whalen, 2021). As an example, Patti's *Olive Garden tweet* has been construed as a dishonest misrepresentation of what machine learning is and how it works (Mandelbaum, 2018).

Bucher has similarly documented the general uproar after it was revealed that an earlier example of bot mimicry, a popular Twitter bot account named *@Horse_ebooks* was in fact driven by a journalist pretending to be a bot (Bucher, 2014). *@Horse_ebooks* was known for tweeting obscure and often seemingly nonsensical snippets of text, and the journalist running the account had to operate a bot-esque style in order to continue the illusion. Much like some of the reactions to Patti's tweet, the responses to the discovery of the humanness of *@Horse_ebooks* prompted mistrust and confusion. As we shall see, these examples of Twitter drama are prefigured by a longer history of machine impersonation that predates the digital computer by centuries.

The hoax of machine impersonation can be understood in the light of impostering. As Vogel et al. point out, the notion of the imposter has often taken the position of the exception to the rule, as a figure that exists on the margins of society. However, by rethinking our understanding of the imposter – and in turn reconsidering our fear of the hoax – we can see that once taken seriously, the imposter offers an operative insight into "the essential indeterminacy" of society (Vogel et al., 2021, p. 5). Bot mimicry embraces indeterminacy inherent to the imposter and the mimic alike, and recognizes that these practices do "not 'just' involve deception, trickery and pretence" (Vogel et al., 2021, p. 3). Rather, they are also illuminative forms of inquiry.

By considering three cases that are all based on deep and imitative engagements with machineries yet are (in different ways) presented as hoaxes, I question the rigidity of the notion of the hoax. Firstly taking on the perhaps most famous case of machine impersonation, namely, the

Mechanical Turk, I locate the origin of the fear of the hoax in the competitive assumptions surrounding the Turk and not least its Enlightenment context. Secondly, I consider a more recent and somewhat less famous example that nonetheless has attained legendary status in the context of generative literature, namely, *The Policeman's Beard is Half Constructed.* This book was an early example of generative literature in book-bound form, and was based on deep engagement with text-generation software, yet this engagement was obscured in the presentation of the book as a wholly computer-generated work – a hoax. Thirdly, and finally, I question the contemporary economic context of bot mimicry, where the labor of so-called microworkers is presented as the output of computer systems. In this context, I locate an artistic intervention in the work *LAUREN*, which shows how bot mimicry can trouble the logic of hoaxing and take the form of inquiry.

2.3.1 The Origins of the Hoax

Although not the earliest, perhaps the most famous example of machine impersonation is the Mechanical Turk. The Mechanical Turk was a chess-playing automaton that gained considerable fame for its ability to beat virtually anyone at the game. The Turk likely inspired Charles Babbage's work on the analytical engine, which, although it was never fully constructed, informed Turing's work and is today considered an industrial precursor of the digital computer (Schaffer, 1999). Likewise, when considering Edgar Allen Poe's famous analysis of the Turk from 1836, wherein Poe argued that the Turk exemplified a case where "what is *merely complex* has been consistently mistaken for what is profound" it becomes clear that it prefigured Alan Turing's conception of the *imitation game* (Ashford, 2017, p. 8). In other words, the Turk is an early example of the tendency to measure (artificial) intelligence on the premise of deception (or hoaxing).

Baron Wolfgang von Kempelen constructed the Mechanical Turk in 1770, and it continued to be in operation for eighty years, even pushing beyond the lifetime of its inventor. The Turk was presented as an automaton, that is, a fully mechanical self-operating construction (what we today would call a robot), but was later revealed to be a hoax: Inside the automaton was a person who, using elaborate control mechanisms and ingeniously placed mirrors, controlled the Turk as a puppet (see Figure 5). The Turk is an early example of an entity that "for some . . . was a machine that displayed remarkably human attributes, while for others, including its designer, it was a human who performed in a strikingly machinelike manner" (Schaffer, 1999, p. 164). The history of imitating and imagining automata goes further back than the Turk (cf. Kang, 2011; cf. Cave et al., 2020). Yet this specific example marks a particularly significant moment that crystallizes a lot of the assumptions that today circulate in the context of imitating imitative software online – including the fear of the hoax.

The Turk instantiated an antagonistic model of humans and machines that continues to inform the notion that bot mimicry is a hoax. It figures as an early example of human/machine antagonism, where human and (mimicked) machine were posed as competitors. On one level, the competition was literal:

Figure 5 An illustration of the Mechanical Turk. *Source:* Wikimedia Commons (von Kempelen).

A game of chess. On another level, there was a more conceptual competition, circulating the Enlightenment imposition of "a division between subjects that could be automated and those reserved for reason" (Schaffer, 1999, p. 164). In other words, the Turk was part of a larger project to determine what *separated* humans (and particularly so-called enlightened humans) from nature (along with the unenlightened and the machinic). Thus audiences would attempt to gauge the inner workings of the Turk, in order to evaluate its status along the enlightened/unenlightened division, unbeknownst that they were gauging the machinic performance of a human puppeteer. Once revealed as a hoax, the Turk reinforced the fear that machines that behaved intelligently were in fact hoaxes. In effect, the Turk would perpetuate a structure of competition and antagonism between humans and machines – an antagonism that continues to inform our understanding of artificial intelligence, as seen most prominently in the standard interpretation of the Turing test, which I will discuss later (cf. Ashford, 2017).

It is telling that the Turk – one of the most influential cases of human/machine antagonism – is actually a case of imitation. Instead of focusing on the audience, who were hoaxed, I am fascinated by the position taken by the person controlling the Turk. What can this puppeteer teach us about the relations between humans and automata in the eighteenth and nineteenth centuries? We have no way of knowing, of course. Instead, we can reorient our focus when considering contemporary practices of bot mimicry, to focus less on the risk of the hoax and more on the imitative position of the mimic themselves. However, when looking at other more recent examples, we can see that the incitement to interpret cases of imitation as hoaxes persists. Even in cases where the operator of a system is engaged in an intimately fluid relation to the computational machinery, there is a drive to present and interpret the situation through the framework of antagonism, in turn reinforcing the unhelpful idea that imitation is the same as hoaxing.

2.3.2 The Incitement to Hoax

The 1984 book *The Policeman's Beard is Half Constructed* was presented as the first ever book written by a computer program, by the name of Racter (short for Raconteur), which was programmed by William Chamberlain and Thomas Etter (Racter et al., 1984). However, it was soon discovered that the book included substantial contributions from Chamberlain and Etter, including curation and editing of the outputs from the Racter. The stylistic touch of human originators of computer program impacted the output to a degree where, as Espen Aarseth (with a reference to Jorn Barger) argues, "the 'wacky' style of Racter's output is really Chamberlain's own, the product of a clever human writer posing as a clever program" (Aarseth, 1997, p. 132; cf. Barger, 1993).

The influence of Chamberlain and Etter notwithstanding, Racter was an important part of the creation of the book. Even though Racter was not stylistically independent, the book was still "one of the first algorithmically authored books" and furthermore an important moment in the "history of algorithmic authorship wherein computer-generated texts became readily available for public consumption" (Henrickson, 2021). Rather than a hoax, we should think of the book as the product of "a cyborg: part Racter, part Chamberlain" (Aarseth, 1997, p. 134). *The Policeman's Beard* is not a case of bot mimicry, but it is informative of the persistence of the concern over the possibility of being hoaxed in cases of bot mimicry.

The resulting style is very close to that of bot mimicry. As Leah Henrickson notes, "Racter's output is always somewhat nonsensical, but the selections comprising *The Policeman's Beard* demonstrate the system's potential for output that might be construed as meaningful" (2021). In this sense, *The Policeman's Beard* displays the recursivity of generative literature and the playful imitation of such literature in the form of bot mimicry: In both cases, the appreciation of the text relies upon the reader's inhibition to construe meaning out of seemingly nonsensical sequences of words.

In spite of the richness of the reciprocity between Racter, Chamberlain, and Etter, the book was presented as the product of Racter's without much mention of the humans in the loop, which can, for example, be seen on the cover where it is marketed as "The First Book Ever Written by a Computer" (see Figure 6). In this way, it becomes a case of an inhibition to present and interpret humans and computers as squarely separable entities instead of highlighting cyborgian moments of reciprocity. By removing the signs of their involvement in the creation of the work,

Chamberlain and Etter exhibit the depth of the culture of hoaxing in questions of text generation.

The contemporary status of the hoax has reached into the heart of the assembly line of artificial intelligence, where the labor of humans is sold as the output of computers, which marks the politico-economic context of bot mimicry. This commodified machine impersonation takes place on micro-work platforms such as the one whose name is inspired by, but which is otherwise not very comparable to, the historical Mechanical Turk – namely, Amazon Mechanical Turk. The important thing here is not the microwork platform in itself, but the curious overlap of humans and computers that emerges in a context that economically exploits the position of standing in a computer's stead. As I will argue, in addition to commodifying bot

Figure 6 Cover of *The Policeman's Beard Is Half Constructed* (Racter et al., 1984).

mimicry, Amazon Mechanical Turk also enables critical-creative experimentation that allows us to understand bot mimicry as inquiry rather than hoax, as encounter rather than conflict.

2.3.3 The Economy of the Hoax

At first sight, the microwork (cf. Irani, 2015) platform Amazon Mechanical Turk is quite far from the practice of bot mimicry – and from the question of hoaxes. The platform even proudly advertises itself as a kind of *artificial artificial intelligence*, boasting the humanity of the workers. Yet upon scrutiny, bot mimicry can be seen to be an idiotic rendering of a social reality for many microworkers who daily stand in computers' stead. Amazon Mechanical Turk (along with other microwork platforms) functions as a crucial part of other services that market themselves as driven by artificial intelligence while using human labor to produce those services. From being one of the main sources of tagging and other categorization used in the creation of datasets used in machine learning systems to outright doing the work of a supposedly artificially intelligent system, these microworkers labor on the assembly lines of our data-driven economy (cf. Tubaro et al., 2020; cf. Pasquinelli and Joler, 2020).

In the platformed economy, human microworkers engage in *artificial intelligence impersonation*, "when humans, so to speak, steal computers' jobs" (Tubaro et al., 2020, p. 7). This is the economic context in which bot mimicry emerges as a techno-cultural practice. The impersonation of artificial intelligence systems by microworkers points to the intensity of the mimetic relation in the platformed context; at no given time does there exist a definite, predefined separation of humans and bots. Bot mimicry can figure as a form of literary and experimental inquiry into the platformed labor conditions of microwork platforms – and into the very relation between humans and nonhumans in platformed contexts.

Consider Lauren Lee McCarthy's 2017 project *LAUREN* (see Figure 7). In this work, McCarthy engages in bot mimicry of a smart home assistant such as Amazon's Alexa. That is to say, McCarthy literally takes on the task of being peoples' smart home assistant, from turning lights on and off, putting on music, and answering queries. LAUREN meditates the conditions of platformed labor, both illuminating the role in which we position our smart home assistants and at the same time providing insight into the position of artificial intelligence impersonation. As such, *LAUREN* also indicates that artificial intelligence impersonation does not only happen on Amazon Mechanical Turk, but also in other lines of platformed work.

As an example, consider Live Eye Surveillance – a surveillance company that employs people to perform the role of monitoring CCTV-cameras that we otherwise increasingly assume are operated by data-driven machine vision technologies. Instead of having a dedicated surveillance unit on location, Live Eye offers a centralized solution where human observers act under the guise of being artificial intelligence-driven. Live Eye almost seems to be a corporate realization of McCarthy's work, which predates the surveillance company – a case of reality imitating the arts? The juxtaposition of McCarthy's artistic bot mimicry and Live Eye's economic model sheds light on the ways in which the boundaries between humans and bots are fading in economic as well as aesthetic contexts – and offers to different approaches to this situation; Live Eye profits from the hoax, whereas McCarthy opts for curious inquiry.

LEARN MORE   LAUREN   GET LAUREN

Figure 7 Lauren Lee McCarthy's *LAUREN* (2017). Reproduced with permission.

2.3.4 Inquiring rather than Hoaxing

In contrast to cases of artificial intelligence impersonation in the platformed labor market, McCarthy does not want to *become* another Alexa; rather, the project is to *encounter* Alexa through imitation. Moreover, McCarthy's project is in part to outperform Alexa – to be more invested, more intuitively attentive than what Amazon can offer. In spite of appearances, this is not only a competitive drive, but also an expression of curiosity and encounter. As McCarthy explains, "[w]hile designing the project, I spent a lot of time thinking about the question, 'If I were an AI, what would I be like?' I tried to create an entity that felt human but could also function like a system" (McCarthy, 2018). By positioning herself as both an imitator and an investigator, McCarthy is harnessing the potential of bot mimicry to function as inquiry into the mimetic assumptions that defines our artificial intelligence imaginaries. In a sense, McCarthy inquires into imitation by way of operating a technique of imitation herself.

In spite of the interest in inquiry, McCarthy somewhat reinforces an antagonistic model of humans and bots in that she moves to outperform Alexa. In Section 3, I discuss the possibility of operating an imitative approach without perpetuating a competitive framework. Still, McCarthy's position shows how imitation can be earnest, and thus illuminates a trajectory for thinking bot mimicry as something other than a hoax. By occupying the position of the bot while remaining open about the mimicry going on, *LAUREN* invites the consideration of the implied bot in practices of bot mimicry without attempting to deceive. Thus *LAUREN* echoes the distinctly *fictional* aspect of bot mimicry outlined earlier – that we need to understand that the implied bot functions with a play on fiction, that it requires us to participate in its imaginative construction. McCarthy's question, "If I were an AI, what would I be like?" is not only to be answered by McCarthy herself, but is also contingent upon *our* understanding of the bot implied in *LAUREN*.

The imaginary aspect of *LAUREN* is based not on a traditional story, but on the consideration of a practice where McCarthy literally takes on the role of a smart home assistant. In this way, *LARUEN* blurs the distinctions between science fact and science fiction, in effect turning our mode of reading bot mimicry into a practice of imaginative prototyping.

2.4 Reading as Prototyping

The case of *LAUREN* leads me to gather the threads of this section, to construct an account of how we can read bot mimicry as a literary practice that is native to the platformed Web and draws on wider techno-cultural dynamics from the history of text generation and the perpetual fear of being hoaxed. Specifically, I argue that it is productive to understand the practice of bot mimicry – and our reading of that practice – in terms of prototyping. The notion of a *diegetic prototype* refers to speculative technologies that belong to a (science fiction) story-world, in which they figure as ordinary things (Kirby, 2010).

In the case of the *Olive Garden tweet*, we might say that the tweet itself, in which Patti claims to have trained a machine learning–based bot on a corpus of Olive Garden commercials, is a short-short science fiction story in itself, and the script is an artifact that should be understood to belong to the diegetic world of that short-short story. Such a reading invites the consideration of – indeed the imaginative co-construction of – the *implied bot itself* in the appreciation of the tweet, rather than (only) focusing on the representation of Olive Garden.

Using diegetic prototypes, designers and researchers can devise plausible, yet fictional, technologies and stage fictional narratives in which the possible techno-cultural consequences of those prototypes play out, which in turn can affect the development of technology beyond the fiction itself (Bleecker, 2009). This practice is known as *design fiction* and allows us to imaginatively inquire into the broader possible impacts of technology. In the case of bot mimicry, the prototyping does not unfold through a traditional narrative: Although the Olive Garden tweet can be read as a short-short story, the script itself and the implied bot responsible for the script are not being narrated to us in a traditional sense – yet both bot and script are fictional, belonging to a fictional world. Rather, the script acts as an *entry point* to a fictional world that is not represented through narrative, but which is still reliant on our imaginations (cf. Coulton et al., 2017). In this way, *reading* bot mimicry becomes an active engagement with *prototyping* – we are not only considering a fictional technology that is narrated to us, we are actively participating in the construction of that very technology.

The reading of bot mimicry entails an engagement with wider techno-cultural structures and must be understood as a reading of an implied technology – which ties onto an artificial intelligence imaginary. In adding the context of design fiction, bot mimicry becomes aligned with a broader consideration of how we can use literary experimentation to rethink the way we design artificial intelligence systems. By considering bot mimicry as a kind of design fiction, in which the bots we mimic take the form of prototypes, the broad possible impact of the new media idiocy of imitating an imaginary shows itself, as it becomes not only a question of what is (or was) trending on Twitter, but an engagement with the broader context of text generation and the concern over the possibility of being hoaxed. In turn, this practice becomes a literary approach to affecting the design of the technologies we encounter every day.

Bot mimicry crystallizes a view into how complex imaginary-induced materialities emerge in and in turn affect digital literary culture. Further, bot mimicry invites a rethinking of some of our most foundational assumptions surrounding artificial intelligence: That imitation is indicative of intelligence. In order to investigate this proposition, we need to further illuminate the issue of imitation in regard to artificial intelligence. Imitation is most often thought of as a drive to fool the observer into thinking the imitator is something they are not by situating a hoax or deceit, but it also carries a poetic potential in situations where the imitator troubles – indeed reverses – the mimetic dynamics at the heart of one of the most foundational ideas surrounding artificial intelligence, namely, the Turing test.

3 Reversing the Imitation Game

The practice of imitating imitative software – bot mimicry – invokes and reverses the dynamics of the *imitation game*, that is, what is now mainly known as the Turing test. In a 1950 paper published in a journal of philosophy, Turing proposed a game to determine a computer's ability to exhibit a "criterion of 'thinking'" (2004, p. 443). The game involves three participants: a (human) interlocutor and two contestants – one computer and one human. The interlocutor should attempt to distinguish the human from the computer by conversing with the two contestants via text only. The human contestant should assist the interlocutor in reaching the correct conclusion, while the computer should seek to imitate the human to such a degree that the judge would make the wrong conclusion.

Turing's criterion of thinking denoted a kind of activity that humans would recognize as thinking. Thus, this criterion was intended to be less loaded than the notion of intelligence; rather than a grand proposal as to the question of intelligence, Turing's imitation game was devised as a measure of what *humans would recognize as* intelligence. Importantly, Turing explicitly noted that there was no reason to believe computers were not already intelligent in ways humans simply could not recognize (2004, p. 442). Since he was interested in the kind of behavior humans would recognize as intelligence, and not intelligence itself, Turing opted for imitation as an ideal measure: if the computer could be made to behave linguistically like a human, then it would have exhibited the criterion of thinking.

Although Turing did not equate his criterion of thinking with intelligence, the imitation game has largely become a central techno-cultural idea pertaining to just that: (artificial) intelligence. Whereas the industry is today largely unconcerned with Turing testing (and opt for other benchmarks), the broader understanding of automated software in society still often circulates Turing's test. This can, for example, be seen in the way we continue to put new text-generation software to the (Turing) test (cf. Elkins and Chun, 2020). Yet while the Turing test is not part of current industry benchmarks, the mimetic dynamic of the imitation game persists. Consider this statement from the developers of a recent artificial intelligence system that has attracted quite some attention: "GPT-3 *improves the quality* of text generation and adaptability ... and *increases the difficulty of distin-guishing* synthetic text from human-written text" (Brown et al., 2020, p. 34, emphasis added). Even if the specific framework of the Turing test is not mentioned, it is clear that *GPT-3* is based on similar assumptions.

Turing published his original paper on the imitation game in a journal of philosophy, and it is indeed the conceptual proposition that there is a connection between thinking and imitation that persists, and not the specific framework of the actual game. It is telling that the quality of a recent artificial intelligence system, *GPT-3*, is determined by the difficulty of distinguishing; this is a clear sign of the centrality of *deception* to our understanding of artificial intelligence. As Simone Natale argues, deception "is as central to [artificial intelligence]'s functioning as the circuits, software, and data that make it run" (2021, p. 2).

We can see the deceptive foundations of the Turing test in the Victorian-era parlor game that served as its inspiration. In the Victorian-era imitation game, an interlocutor would try to distinguish a man from a woman, with the man trying to fool the interlocutor to make the wrong guess and the woman assisting the interlocutor in reaching the right conclusion. In turn, Turing proposed that the computer should take the place of the man in this setup, thus implying that the test for the criterion of thinking relied on the computer's ability to perform not just as any human, but specifically as man pretending to be a woman. The strangely gendered aspect of Turing's proposal is complicated further by the fact that Turing himself was queer in a society where homosexuality was criminalized, and as such also had to play a kind of imitation game, attempting to perform the role of a straight man. Once Turing's queerness was discovered, he was subjected to chemi-cal castration and eventually died by suicide. As a queer pioneer of computing (cf. Blas and Cárdenas, 2013), Turing himself suffered the worst possible consequences of failing a game of imitation. Noting the parallel between the imitation required by computers and the issue of Turing's own imitation of a sexuality foreign to him, Benjamin Bratton argues that "[t]he demands of both bluffs are unnecessary and profoundly unfair" (2015, p. 72).

The requirement of bluffing, fooling, or deceiving the interlocutor implies an anthropomorphic imaginary of artificial intelligence (Bratton,

2015; Goffey, 2008). By focusing on the assessment made by the interlocutor, the imitation game positions the human at the center of the question of artificial intelligence. Further, as Brian Christian shows in *The Most Human Human*, the imitation game might principally be a setup for investigating what it means to be human, rather than what artificial intelligence is. Christian focuses on Loebner Prize competition, a manifestation of the Turing test in which a number of bot creators compete to create the most convincingly humanlike bot, as judged by a panel of experts. Entering into the competition as a human confederate meant to be the scale against which the competing bots are evaluated, Christian has to take care to perform in an as humanlike manner as possible, to give the bots adequate competition. Christian succeeds to the point of being awarded the prize as the most human human – the human confederate who was ranked as most humanlike by the panel.

Christian illuminates his performance as the most human human in the Loebner Prize competition as a study of what it even means to be – and perform as – humans vis-à-vis automated software. Christian's project shows the mimetic reciprocity of humans and bots – learning about one also affords insight into the other – yet it also buttresses an antagonistic relation between these mimetic counterparts. By seeking to outdo his bot competitors, Christian only learns about them in order to defeat them, asserting that the presence of bots on the platformed Web means that "[a]ll communication is suspect," given that any interaction might involve malicious bots (Christian, 2011, p. 9). In this way Christian's project shows how an anthropomorphic approach of bots also invites an antagonistic assumption.

The antagonism between humans and computers implies an understanding of computers as being *automative*, that is, fundamentally independent of humans (Schwartz, 2018). The automative imaginary presupposes an accumulation of computing power that leads to a moment when computers surpass humans and become capable of self-improvement (Good, 1966). Although there is some disagreement as to whether such self-improving computers would mean the salvation or doom of humanity, proponents of the automative imaginary tend to agree that once computers reach a self-improving state, they will be fundamentally independent.

The anthropomorphic and automative imaginaries of artificial intelligence often coexist, meaning that there is an assumption that artificial intelligence will be completely independent of humans, however only insofar as it behaves in a way that humans recognize as being intelligent. The automative imaginary mobilizes the indistinguishability of humans from computers as a threshold for artificial intelligence, yet also curiously builds on the belief that once such a threshold has been passed, the artificially intelligent system will be fundamentally independent of humans. According to Oscar Schwartz, the automative assumption is directly traceable to the imitation game, just as Bratton and Andrew Goffey both trace our anthropomorphic assumptions regarding artificial intelligence to Turing's work. In effect, we are dealing with an amalgamated *anthropomorphic and automative imaginary of artificial intelligence*. Rather than understanding this imaginary as being inherent to Turing's work, however, I consider it to be a morphed operationalization of the imitation game that might be traceable, but in no way reducible, to Turing's original proposal. In fact, the main point of this section is to reconsider the anthropomorphic and automative imaginary that, although dominant, is not irrevocable.

Both the anthropomorphic and the automative imaginaries of artificial intelligence are derived from a standard interpretation of the imitation game. This interpretation focuses on imitation only as means to or measure of intelligence, and not as an end, or an object of interest, in itself. In arguing that we should move away from the imitative structure, critics of the imitation game do not sufficiently question the equivocation of imitation and intelligence – by contrast, they reinforce it. Instead of rejecting the imitation, and thus inadvertently reinforcing the equivocation of imitation and intelligence, I move to reconsider the imitative dynamic itself, to rework it through engagement rather than rejection, to renegotiate the situation by mimicking it differently. However, instead of seeking to move away from imitation in the consideration of artificial intelligence, I propose to move critically *into* the imitation. That we begin considering imitation as a significant phenomenon in its own right. As I will argue, there is much more nuance and friction to be found in the imitation game than what immediately meets the eye, particularly upon reversing its dynamics.

Bot mimicry can be understood as a reversal of the imitation game – one that troubles both the anthropomorphic and the automative assumptions so often associated with the Turing test. To the end of investigating this claim, I analyze two creative platforms for alternative imitation games, setting the stage for a formulation of a reverse imitation game that characterizes the dynamics of bot mimicry. These two cases, respectively *BotPoet* and *BotorNot*, draw on and frame themselves in relation to the historical imitation game, yet they also diverge therefrom, and add valuable dimensions to the study of how the imitation game informs the way we read and write vis-à-vis bots.[2] In my proxy-analysis of the imitation game through the selected cases, I opt for an approach that goes *against* the dominant interpretation of the imitation game. I move to illuminate the imitation game as a cultural arena in which we may encounter, rather than compete against, our automated counterparts.

3.1 Reading (against) an Imitation Game

> This website is a Turing test for poetry. You, the judge, have to guess whether the poem you're reading is written by a human or by a computer. (Schwartz and Laird, n.d.)

Upon loading the *BotPoet* website, one is met with the statement quoted above.[3] The statement is followed by the elaboration that "[i]f you think a poem was written by a computer, choose 'bot'. If you think it was written by a human, choose 'not'" (Schwartz and Laird, n.d.). If we wonder what kinds of poems get to count as either human-written or computer-generated,

---

[2] Both of these websites bear the name 'Bot or Not'. In order to ease the distinction between them, I rename them in a way that is inspired by their respective URLs: *BotPoet*, based on the URL www.BotPoet.com; and *BotorNot*, loosely based on the URL www.botor.no.

[3] The *BotPoet* website is no longer available on its original URL, but it has been archived by the Internet Archive, securing access to most parts of the website. Some of the website's interactive aspects do not work in its archived state, but the parts that are relevant to my analysis (principally the leaderboard page) can still be accessed. https://web.archive.org/web/20200116213612/http://botpoet.com/.

BotPoet provides a provisional definition of computer poetry, stating that "computer poetry uses algorithms to generate text," yet maintains that "specific criteria for computer poetry is [*sic*] flexible" (Schwartz and Laird, n.d.). Conversely, human poetry is defined as "[e]verything else ... " (Schwartz and Laird, n.d.).

The website frames itself as a Turing test, yet it also diverges from Turing's original proposition in some important ways. When playing the *BotPoet* game, one is presented with a poem and faced with a choice – to assert via abduction – whether a human or a computer wrote the poem. There is no option to converse with or inquire further into the originator of the poem, only the choice between "bot" and "not." In short, *BotPoet* transforms the role of the interlocutor to that of a judge – and, ultimately, a *reader*. Still, *BotPoet* preserves the setup of the Turing test in many other ways, most notably in the general framework of asking a human to distinguish humans from computers based on textual output. I here focus on the way *BotPoet* illuminates the position of the judge – the reader – in relation to the imitation game, in order to gauge the characteristics of the kind of reading we engage in when we encounter bots online.

The first inhibition of the reader on the *BotPoet* platform is to attempt to distinguish bot poems from human poems. Over time, however, instead of improving our skills at the game the result is actually quite the opposite: The more we play, the more we become aware that it is pragmatically impossible to reliably get the correct answer – no matter how good a sense of bot literacy we possess. There seems to be a kind of equilibrium, at least on the side of the reading, between bot poets and human poets. In other words, John Irving Good's (1966) speculation that poetry would be an indicator of ultra-intelligent machines seems to have been met (1966, p. 36).

However, instead of professing that machines are now ultra-intelligent, perhaps we need to reconfigure our belief that poetry is as human as we have tended to believe. It is telling that the top-ranking poem of the "most computer-like human poems" category in *BotPoet*'s accompanying *leaderboard* subpage is from Gertrude Stein's *Tender Buttons* (2005), which was written several decades before Turing's advent of the imitation game, and before the creation of the first digital computers. Perhaps (at least some) human poetry is not that humanlike after all. Can we move further into this overlap of humans and bots that trouble the antagonistic structure of the imitation game? Can we locate nuance and friction by reading *against* this poetically inclined Turing test?

Although *BotPoet* includes a large amount of individually interesting poems that reside in and illuminate the friction-filled space between human-like and bot-esque writing, I turn to focus not so much on individual poems as on the platform of BotPoem itself. The drive to distinguish humans from bots based on individual text snippets is – at least in the domain of poetry – less than productive to the investigation of bot mimicry. Yet the aforementioned leaderboard may afford a more productive way of reading the *BotPoet* platform. The leaderboard subpage makes it possible for users to monitor a top-five ranking in four categories: *most human-like human poems*, *most human-like computer poems*, *most computer-like computer poems*, and *most computer-like human poems*. The leaderboard provides a useful case for the question of reading, since it affords a kind of datafied, amalgamated perspective on how users of *BotPoet* tend to judge poems. As such, it invites us to also consider our reading of bots online as less a question of individual exchanges, but as parts of a larger – datafied – whole.

Our engagements with bots are not just our own; they also rely on, and feed into, data practices. This means that whenever we encounter a poem (computer-generated or not) online, "[t]he datafication of reader response *is an essential part of the poem*, one whose effects are visible to readers only indirectly in ads prompted by the reader's engagement with the poem" (Berens, 2019, original emphasis). Thus, a software-sensitive way of reading poetry on the platformed web becomes a practice of "skimming the content and close reading the promiscuous read/write capacities of social media metadata, and guessing at the black-boxed code" (Berens, 2019). In the case of *BotPoet*, the data is (to my knowledge) not brokered to third parties, and so the datafication of our reading experience is not visible in ads, but it is made available to us in the leaderboard.

The leaderboard leads me to the relation between *BotPoet* and the practice of bot mimicry. Specifically, the category of *most computer-like human poems* instantiates this relation, along with that category's comparative difference to the two other categories of *most human-like human poems* and *most computer-like computer poems* (see Figure 8). Even though these

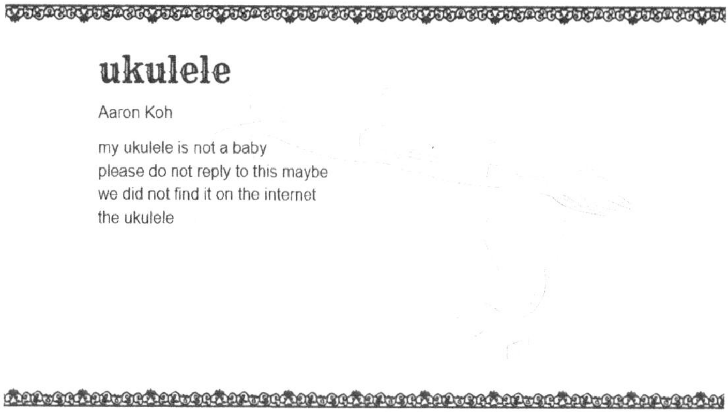

ukulele

Aaron Koh

my ukulele is not a baby
please do not reply to this maybe
we did not find it on the internet
the ukulele

Figure 8 An example of a poem featured on the BotPoet website. Taking the third place in the *most computer-like human poetry*, 68 percent of players wrongly guess that this poem was written by a bot (Schwartz and Laird, n.d.). Reproduced with permission.

categories seem like (and are presented as) distinct from each other, the similarity between the two *most computer-like* categories points toward the mimetic reciprocity of the categories. Un-black-boxing at least some of the data gathered from reader interaction, the leaderboard section invites the reader to consider the broader scope of the platform, not just the singular poems. Although we may navigate to some of the poems featured in the leaderboard out of curiosity, the interest in the singular poem quickly fades. Instead, what emerges is a curiosity toward the messiness and overlap of human and computer writing across poems and categories. Instead of reading the poems with a competitive mindset, we can approach them as spaces for literary encounter with our automated counterparts.

BotPoet establishes an opportunity for reading against the standard interpretation of the imitation game, which takes us down other relational avenues vis-à-vis bots. However, this platform importantly only pertains to reading. Bot mimicry is principally a practice of *writing*, which I will turn to in the following.

3.2 Writing (against) an Imitation Game

> Potentially matched to either a bot or a person, players are forced to
> question not only the human-ness of their opponent, but also themselves
> as they engage in a two-way guessing game. (Foreign Objects, n.d.a)

BotorNot is an online conversational game that resembles a Turing test in
many ways while, as is evident in the quote above, aiming at the didactic
goal of "engag[ing] people in thinking critically about artificial agents
that pretend to be human" (Foreign Objects, n.d.a). *BotorNot* describes
itself as "a kind of Turing test" (Foreign Objects, n.d.b), yet the
objective of the game is not to inquire into the intelligence of computers.
Rather, the game's goal is to teach the player some significant ways in
which bots currently attempt to (dishonestly) pose as humans. The
premise for the *BotorNot* game is thus a certain suspicion toward bots
per se, posing these systems as dishonest and dangerous, exemplified by
"scam bots on Tinder and Instagram, or corporate bots that steal your
data" (Foreign Objects, n.d.b). The importance of making people aware
of the malicious aspects of some bots notwithstanding, I am here in
search of other ways of relating to bots that instantiate alternatives to
suspicion. As I will argue, *BotorNot* can indeed provide a framework for
poetic as well as critical experiences and practices that make way for
curiosity rather than only suspicion. Whereas the website frames itself as
a pathway to become critical of bots, I approach it as a space for
experimental writing. In other words, I aim to uncover ways of writing
against this didactically oriented Turing test.

   BotorNot preserves many features from Turing's historical proposal with
an important modification: the game is played with only two participants
interrogating and judging each other. On the side of the one player, the
question becomes to decide if the *other player* is a bot or a human – instead of
the standard requirement to distinguish between two different contestants.
We might say that in *BotorNot*, the three roles from Turing's imitation
game – (human) interlocutor, human contestant, and computer contestant –
conflate into two: interlocutor-human and interlocutor-computer OR interlocutor-human.

The structure of the game is inspired by the popular social game *truth or dare* (specifically its *truth*-aspect), where each player takes turns presenting the other with *truth challenges*. The game has four rounds: first, a one-minute round for introductions, followed by three one-minute rounds of truth challenges. Turing's original test had a five-minute interaction as a proposed timeframe, which almost corresponds to *BotorNot*'s four minutes. A notable difference in terms of structure is that the interaction is cut into smaller portions and framed within the context of truth challenges, which is a way to narrow down the scope of the conversation, unlike Turing's emphasis that the interlocutor should be able to inquire into any topic of their choosing.

BotorNot does not come with an un-black-boxed insight into the datafication going on akin to *BotPoet*'s leaderboard (it does state that user interactions are not tracked, so perhaps there are none). The comparative lack of a leaderboard (or something similar) further solidifies that *BotorNot* in no way aims at testing the intelligence of the bot. On the contrary, *BotorNot* seems more like a place to test and hone the human's bot-detection skills. This notion is strengthened in that the player is always paired with the same bot. I have played the game a lot, and although I cannot be absolutely certain that the bot I am matched to is completely the same in terms of programming, it is clear to me from my playthroughs that all the bots I have been paired with operate the same conversational logic. By this I mean that they ask the same kinds of questions (sometimes word for word) and furthermore answer in similar ways (again, sometimes word for word). Indeed, as we play the game multiple times, we get an almost intimate understanding of our bot counterpart. This in spite of the fact that, according to the *BotorNot* website, its goal is not to provide an opportunity to acquaint ourselves with the specific bot from the game, but to facilitate critical thinking. The idea seems to be that a person plays the game only once or twice, is struck by critical thought, and immediately moves to read the supplementary and in many ways quite useful text, *A Guide for the Bot Curious*, written by the developers of the game Foreign Objects.

In their presentation of the issue of automated software, Foreign Objects focus on the dangers of broad implementation of bots, and on the importance of being able to distinguish bots from humans. As we saw in the case of *BotPoet* earlier, though, the development of such bot-detection skills may be of little use in situ – and the futility of attempting to distinguish humans from computers solely based on text is rapidly increasing. However, in their guide for the bot curious, Foreign Objects do touch upon some of the issues that I am also investigating here: "[A]s chatbots become increasingly human-like, we too begin to question the terms of our own humanness in exciting, revealing and troubling ways" (Foreign Objects, n.d.c). This inhibition to turn the imitation game into an introspection echoes Christian's efforts to be recognized as the most human human (Christian, 2011). If, instead of seeking to improve our abilities to detect bots, we embrace the fluidity of human and computer writing and begin experimenting, *BotorNot* might be an optimal place through which to use writing as inquiry into the intense mimetic reciprocity of humans and computers. One approach could be to reproduce the bot-esque writing style found in *r/totallynotrobots* in conversation with the BotorNot bot (see Figure 9). Perhaps there is value in inverting the call to "act human!" and instead act computationally (Foreign Objects, n.d.b).

Whether we attempt to act human or computationally – whether we experiment with our humanity or with the mimetic reciprocity of ourselves and our bot counterpart – we do so comparatively, vis-à-vis our fellow bot (or not). It is here that the importance of writing comes to the fore: *BotorNot* instantiates the imitation game not just as a measure of how you read, but also of how you are read, based on the things you write. In my experience, the way I wrote on the platform changed when I noticed that I always seemed to be paired with a bot (indeed, as mentioned, the same bot), and *never* a human. The lack of humans may be a consequence of the game's relative obscurity, meaning that it may not be popular enough to attract a stable crowd of players, especially in my (continental European) time zone. Put differently, there may simply not be any other humans with whom to be paired. However, I am compelled to also entertain the possibility that there is no actual option to be paired with a human, but we are merely being falsely led to believe so by the website. The question of the actual possibility of being paired with a human notwithstanding, the clear tendency in my many bot encounters makes it clear that we should at least not expect anything but a bot (and the same bot) to be on the other end. In

PLAYING WITH MIKE 00:01

ahhh

what does your tinder profile say?

do bots have sex?

It says "HELLO! I AM A FELLOW HUMAN LOOKING FOR ROMANTIC ENCOUNTERS"

awwwwwww

lol.

• ••

Say something...

Figure 9 A screenshot of one of my many conversations on the *BotorNot* website (Foreign Objects, n.d.b). Reproduced with permission.

other words, we are writing not to be read by a human, but to be read by a bot.

When facing *BotorNot*, we might then take to writing in an experimental way, questioning our humanity and inquiring into our bot counterpart. We might write obscurely, and be amused at the kinds of responses we get. We might write earnestly, and read our bot's responses equally earnestly. Or we might write in a bot-esque manner, entering into the conversation with our bot counterpart on the premises of their style and rhetoric. Even though these options (and there are undoubtedly more that I have not considered here) seem to be of equal value in our exploring our own humanity, the last one – adopting the style and rhetoric of our bot counterpart – contains potentials for new ways of knowing about our particular bot counterpart, but also about the relation between and overlap of our humanity and the bot's computationality.

In the following, I consider the implications of my two analyses of creative imitation games, wherein I have investigated ways of reading and writing *against* the standard interpretation of the imitation game. As it turns out, the relation between my analyses and the standard interpretation of the imitation game circulates a dynamic of *boringness*.

3.3 Formulating the Reverse Imitation Game of Bot Mimicry

BotPoet and *BotorNot* are two examples of creative Turing tests that, if approached with the anthropomorphic and automative imaginary of the standard interpretation of the imitation game in mind, are actually quite boring. Indeed, the proposition that anyone might want to engage with *BotorNot* more than once (or maybe more than twice, seeing that only on the second playthrough would the repetitiveness become truly apparent) appears less than likely. *BotorNot*, with all its emphasis on critical thinking, is quite dull if played according to its own setup. Likewise, the leaderboard section of *BotPoet* may lead us to disregard the gamified aspects of that website altogether – to abandon the effort to distinguish bot from not seeing that the work has already been done, and anyway, there seems to be little that can be done to increase our success rate at the game. It is, however, in their very boringness that they reveal something about the excitement of bot mimicry. In the context of the platformed Web, where "a rule for virality is entertainment . . . tweaking those rules to make something really *boring* may expose a productive political tension" (Saum-Pascual, 2020, emphasis added). In other words, in a world of entertainment, boringness becomes friction, which in turn unveils something significant about the constructs that made the boring thing boring in the first place. How far does the boringness go?

As it turns out, it is not just *BotPoet* and *BotorNot* that are boring: the very advent of the imitation game seems to be quite boring in itself. From a literary perspective, computational imitation of humanlike text seems to only produce clichéd language, and to largely forgo the opportunity to radically rethink what literature is and can be. The boringness of Turing testing reveals a certain *anxiety of imitation*, a reluctance to enter into the imitative dynamic based on the notion that it limits or disables the vibrancy of literary experimentation (Booten and Rockmore, 2020). Yet if we – in the spirit of my readings of *BotPoet* and *BotorNot* – reframe our understanding of the imitative dynamic, we can see that imitation is in fact in itself a vibrant mode of experimenting with the similarities, differences, and nuances between human writing and computational text generation, emphasizing the poetic aspects of imitative computation beyond the question of whether human poets are replaceable by machines.

The interest here is not in the success or failure of a given system – not in the result of the imitation – but in the imitation itself. In this sense, we should think of the imitation game not as a platform to test computers' anthropomorphism, but as "an opportunity to confront our own definitions of human thought in order to see – to *test* – where they may indeed overlap with and diverge from machine cognition" (Booten and Rockmore, 2020, original emphasis). Bot mimicry, then, is a way to engage creatively and curiously in such confrontation through the literary and mimetic technology of writing: by reversing, instead of rejecting, the imitation game.

Moving along this line of thinking, we may ask: What if we reversed the mimetic dynamics, so that the human was to imitate the computer? Turing did, in fact, consider such a reversal, but found it somewhat absurd: "If the man were to try and pretend to be the machine he would clearly make a very poor showing. He would be given away at once by slowness and inaccuracy in arithmetic" (2004, p. 442). Surely, Turing was right in this regard – no human could ever reproduce the speed and accuracy of computers in terms of mathematics; that is, no human could succeed in imitating a computer *as such*. In order to be more worthwhile, the proposed reversal of the imitation game should keep the focus on the hybridity of humans and computers beyond measuring the success of one on the participants over the other: What if the human was to imitate a computer *that imitated a human*? This double imitation is aligned with the definition of bot mimicry. In this version, the computer would try to imitate a human while the human would perform bot mimicry.

The reversed imitation game does still, however, preserve a competitive structure, which is not productive to the endeavor of bot mimicry – even if it makes sense in other contexts in which the imitation game exists. As the analysis of *BotPoet* earlier shows, leaving behind our focus on competition makes us more attuned to the possibilities of encounter. Thus, a more productive reversal of the imitation game would entail engaging in bot mimicry without the formalized structure of a judge whose goal is one of distinction. This does not mean that such a practice would be unconcerned with its readers and possible readings, but, rather, that the relationship to the reader is one of critical creativity and community rather than separation and antagonism.

The reversal of the imitation game, with the added double imitation and the removal of the competitive structure, does not negate that bot mimicry still works as and with a play on deception. Although, as I have argued earlier, bot mimicry should principally be understood as inquiry rather than hoax, the practice still connects to what Natale conceptualizes as *banal deception*. As Natale argues, all perception is potentially deceptive – there are also multiple ways of looking (literally and figuratively) at a situation, any of which could potentially turn out to be a case of deceit. Banal deception, then, is the tendency of users "to embrace deception so that they can better incorporate [artificial intelligence] into their everyday lives, making [it] more meaningful and useful to them" (Natale, 2021, p. 7). In turn, bot mimicry can be understood as a literary engagement with banal deception: A curious playfulness that operates in a deceptive framework without being maliciously deceptive itself.

So what kinds of knowing – about any particular AI-system and/or about our relation to AIs in general – are instantiated in the banal deception of bot mimicry? By building on and reworking (reversing) the imitation game in this way, might we begin to make our understanding of automated computational agents more attuned to the nuances that we cannot *think* but that we might still be able to *know*? In the following section, I take on these questions in through the *instantaneous flash* of recognition of *nonsensuous similarities* that is invigorated in what Walter Benjamin called *the mimetic faculty*.

4 An Awakening of the Mimetic Faculty

At this point, the Element changes its register slightly: Instead of continuing to focus on the various backgrounds and contexts of bot mimicry, I turn to inquire more directly into its mimetic dynamic. Specifically, this section will illuminate how bot mimicry awakens and harnesses *the mimetic faculty* as the driver that materializes – and makes malleable – our artificial intelligence imaginaries through the practice of bot mimicry.

Walter Benjamin developed the theory of the mimetic faculty over the course of four short and only posthumously published essay fragments from the early 1930s (Benjamin, 1999a, 1999b, 1999c, 1999d). In short, this theory concerns human perception and stages mimetic ways of knowing which offers valuable insight into the mimetic dynamics of bot mimicry. Roughly sixty years after Benjamin's fragmented conception of the mimetic faculty, Michael Taussig took up and reworked the theory in a study of indigenous peoples' usage of mimicry in the resistance to enforced colonial assimilation. In this section, I once again take up the concept to consider in a new context and a new time. The concept enables a theoretical account of the centrality of mimicry to perception and to language, and is informative of the more specific workings of bot mimicry.

It is possible to locate other theoretical sources to illuminate the mimetic dynamics at play in these cases – Benjamin is not alone in illuminating the specificities of mimicry. As one example, Jane Bennett's concept of *sympathy* is relevant, since it establishes how mimicry can instantiate a "more-than-human flow of communicative transfers" between and across humans and nonhumans, working akin to an atmospheric force (2020, p. 29). I have explored Bennett's theory of sympathy in relation to bot mimicry elsewhere (Erslev, 2022), and while I note its relevance I will not explore it in depth here. Instead, my exploration of the mimetic faculty aims to work in tandem with contemporary work on the subject of mimicry, such as Bennett's sympathy or Goriunova's idiocy (discussed earlier), to explore the mimetic nuances of our current techno-cultural moment.

Building on the theory of the mimetic faculty, this section offers a more detailed account of how and by what means bot mimicry renders artificial intelligence imaginaries and makes them negotiable in and through digital literary culture. I base my investigation of the role of the mimetic faculty in bot mimicry on a reading specific case, namely *r/totallynotrobots* (read: totally not robots), which is an online community hosting thousands of people in a continuous, distributed, and open-ended performance of bot mimicry. The first part of the section focuses on Benjamin's own formulation of the mimetic faculty, operating Benjamin's original formulation of the concept in an investigation of how bot mimicry renders imaginaries through language play. The second part of the section continues the investigation to focus more on the mimetic agency afforded in practices of mimicry by bringing in Taussig's reworking of Benjamin's theory, in effect illuminating how bot mimicry makes imaginaries not only visible, but also malleable.

The point of this section, then, is to further investigate the relation between literary playfulness and the perception of artificial intelligence imaginaries. Importantly, bot mimicry should be understood not in terms of *what it says* about artificial intelligence imaginaries, but *how it says what it says*. As I will argue, bot mimicry works via the appreciation of *nonsensuous similarities* between a bot-esque style and our artificial intelligence imaginaries that act as "stimulants and awakeners of the mimetic faculty" in the twenty-first century (Benjamin, 1999c, p. 720).

4.1 Greetings Fellow Humans!

Such is one welcomed to the subreddit *r/totallynotrobots*, a community that (at the time of writing) has about 400,000 members and has been active since 2015. A subreddit is a smaller community within the larger platform Reddit, dedicated to a specific topic. All of Reddit is segmented into subreddits, which means that there is no activity on Reddit that is not tied to one or more subreddit(s). The subreddit is at first sight a strange performative community, in which everyone writes in uppercase, primarily in a semantically confusing and syntactically roundabout way. When at times someone (usually an outsider, unfamiliar with the community and its style) posts in lowercase or writes in a straightforward fashion, the other users will demonstrate confusion and seem to worry. They might ask why the user is "yelling" – referring to their use of lowercase – or inquire into semantically banal but syntactically ambiguous statements in the outsider's post. Most of the posts by regular users consist of content shared from other places on the internet (often from other subreddits), accompanied by a bot-esque tagline, explaining the relevancy of the shared content in the style of the community.

What looks like a confusing and unwelcoming community of users writing syntactically strange and Caps-Locked posts is, to my knowledge, also the largest and most long-lived performance of bot mimicry. The *r/totallynotrobots* community is strikingly consistent in terms of style of writing, despite being as open to participation as it is. The writing style appeals just enough for a broad crowd to allow people to creatively join the conversation through their *mimetic faculty* (introduced below), yet specialized enough for the community to sustain a consistent style. As a defining feature, the *r/totallynotrobots* community features a rich comment section in which other users respond to, rephrase, or further develop the humorous content in the main posts of the subreddit. The comment sections sustain a distributed and dialogic performance of bot mimicry where each post does not exist in isolation but must be considered in light of the proceedings in the comments.

The popularity of *r/totallynotrobots* is testimony to the broad reach of bot mimicry as a practice that derives from and flourishes in quotidian contexts, making it popular as it is ripe with poetic and techno-cultural potency. In the following, I introduce the concept of nonsensuous similarity, which is at the center of the theory of the mimetic faculty, and which is useful to unravel the mimicry of *r/totallynotrobots*.

4.2 Nonsensuous Similarity

The word "onomatopoeia" is an onomatopoeia because it is derived from the sound it makes when the word is spoken out loud.

The quote above is taken from a legendary new media idiot (cf. section 2), namely, the user *Ken M*. Although Ken M is most commonly referred to as a troll (cf. Spool, 2015), I consider new media idiocy a more fitting term, since Ken M is rarely, if ever, engaged in transgressive behavior, but always (new media) idiotic. This quote was lifted from a screenshot of a comment section on Yahoo News, posted to the *r/KenM* subreddit (HeimrArnadalr, 2018), and serves to instantiate the unlikely connection between new media idiocy on internet platforms and a series of unfinished fragments from the 1930s detailing a theory of a mimetic faculty and its role in our appreciation of linguistic meaning.

Before applying the theory of the mimetic faculty to the phenomenon of bot mimicry, it is useful to consider the theory itself in some detail. Seeing as how this theory has not previously been introduced into the study of digital culture, some slowness of progression is necessary, to the end of situating a careful integration of the theory into the context of this study and in order to enable other scholars in digital culture to draw on what can be considered "the definitive statement of [Benjamin's] philosophy of experience" (Ogden, 2010, p. 57).

Benjamin's writings on the mimetic faculty coincide with a shift in his intellectual orientation. His early writings on language are somewhat mystical, placing words' meanings and our appreciation thereof in a religious, transcendental context. By contrast, his later thinking aligns with materialist assumptions. As Anson Rabinbach notes, it is possible to track Benjamin's drift from mystical to materialist thinking in his writings on the mimetic faculty. Whereas "Doctrine of the Similar" expresses a reliance on mysticism, "On the Mimetic Faculty" deemphasizes the relation between language and magic (see Rabinbach, 1979, p. 62). I align myself with the latter – materialist – tendency in Benjamin's thinking. Still, I draw on the earlier fragments on the mimetic faculty as well, including their discussions of magic. As Richard Wolin (1982) argues, it would be faulty to detach Benjamin's early mysticism from his later insights – they are instrumental to the vibrancy of his thinking. This does not mean we should take Benjamin's discussions of magic at face value and perpetuate religious mysticism. Instead, it means that adequately understanding the applicability of Benjamin's later materialist thinking requires us also to consider his early, more mystical musings – with a critical awareness of their status as such.

The central concept in the theory of the mimetic faculty is *nonsensuous similarity*, that is, a conception of those instances where there exists a striking similarity between two entities that are *sensuously* dissimilar. Put differently, the mimetic faculty is at play in those cases where we perceive a similarity yet cannot explain it by pointing to the physical manifestations of the nonsensuously similar entities. The nonsensuous does not necessarily stand in opposition to the sensuous; instead, the nonsensuous is that which always has the potential to become sensuous (via the mimetic faculty) and which emerges as "the surplus values of [the sensuous'] various ways of exceeding itself" (Massumi, 2014, p. 67). As one example of nonsensuous similarity, Benjamin mentions constellations of stars: although there is little sensuous similarity between the scattered dots in the sky and the mythical figure of Orion, our mimetic faculties allow us to perceive the surplus value of the sensuous dots in order for Orion to appear. The claim here is that identifying the constellation of Orion in the sky is not just a cognitive process of understanding that certain stars represent Orion in an abstract way. Rather, it is an aesthetic process: we literally see Orion (while also simply seeing a number of dots).

Benjamin's prime example of contemporary nonsensuous similarity is not constellations but language. Instead of viewing our tendency to perceive similarities in sensuously dissimilar phenomena as a result of cognitive bias or a psychoanalytically explainable projection, Benjamin positions nonsensuous similarity at the center of experience as such: Not as a bug but as a feature. The mimetic faculty, and nonsensuous similarity, is thus not only at work in cases of overt imitation, but in all mental activities, seeing as "there may be no single of [human beings'] higher functions that is not codetermined by the mimetic faculty" (Benjamin, 1999d, p. 694).

The mimetic faculty has a history; it is not static but morphs in tandem with cultural changes over the course of millennia. In (pre-)Antiquity, the mimetic faculty might have been openly at play in some of the most vital moments in both cultural and personal life, exemplified by the practice of astrology, where cosmos, society, and person were thought to align in reciprocal mimicry, situated around the reading of constellations of stars (Benjamin, 1999a). Today, however, the mimetic faculty has a different role in society: we tend to think of mimicry as something that mainly pertains to children's play and not as anything of greater societal importance. As a consequence, our current ability to perceive similarities "is nothing but a rudiment of the once powerful compulsion to become similar and to behave mimetically" (Benjamin, 1999c, p. 720). However, as Benjamin argues, we are not dealing with a decrease in the importance of the mimetic faculty to personal or societal issues, but with a transformation in respect to how the mimetic faculty works. Instead of being openly mimetic, we are today dealing with a mode of experience determined by a hidden, or nonsensuous, working of the mimetic faculty. This means that "the cases in which [we] consciously perceive similarities in everyday life make up a tiny proportion of those numberless cases unconsciously determined by similarity" (Benjamin, 1999d, pp. 694–695).

4.2.1 Language as Onomatopoeia

Benjamin argues that language is "the most complete archive of nonsensuous similarity: a medium into which the earlier powers of mimetic production and comprehension have passed without residue" (Benjamin, 1999c, p. 722).

The role of nonsensuous similarities in language can be understood vis-à-vis the notion of *onomatopoeia*, that is, words that sound like what they mean, such as the word *SPLASH*, which is derived from an attempt to mimic the sound of, well, a splash. Onomatopoeias are *sonically* mimetic in that they imitate the sounds they denote, but they are not necessarily mimetic in the more traditional sense of being realistic, as it were. In other words, onomatopoeias are mimetic in a material way, and their meaning cannot be separated from their pronunciation.

Benjamin broadens the sonically and materially mimetic nature of onomatopoeias and uses it as a prism through which we can understand our aesthetic appreciation of linguistic signs (written and/or spoken). The central insight is that in our appreciation of language, the mimetic faculty situates and aesthetic experience of the sign that gives rise to a surplus value that exceeds (and in a sense mediates) the meaning of it. This is a different understanding of mimetic language than the more conventional use of the term as referring to realism. Instead of being mimetic in the sense that the meaning corresponds to our understanding of reality, the concept of nonsensuous similarities in language asserts that before we can even make such a judgment, the mimetic faculty has already been in play in our very appreciation of the signs themselves.

The play of nonsensuous similarities in can serve to explain why the use of language is not just a matter of finding technically equivalent words.

Even if I am referring to the same thing, it matters what I call it: bot, robot, artificial intelligence, automated software, nonhuman, and so on. I have earlier noted that I mostly use "bot" as a catch-all that in many cases includes more than one, if not all, of the notions listed. My amalgamation of words notwithstanding, it is significant that I specifically choose "bot" as my catch-all, since this Element would read quite differently if I used "nonhuman" instead of "bot" throughout. This goes on to say that words and their meanings become entangled through their nonsensuous connectedness. This entanglement goes both ways – it is not just the case that my choice of words affects my own and other human's ability to understand a static entity that is separated from the language used to denote it, but rather that the words we use and the things we use words about are intertwined so that playing with language is also a form of inquiry into materiality.

Benjamin argues that nonsensuous similarities are at play in both written and oral language; in both cases, the perception of the word is inseparable from the appreciation of its meaning. Form and content become inseparable by their mimetic relation. Rather than separating the moment of reading or listening to the form of a word and the moment of understanding its content, the perception of language is "in every case bound to a flashing up. It flits past, can possibly be won again, but cannot really be held fast as can other perceptions. It offers itself to the eye as fleetingly and transitorily as a constellation of stars" (Benjamin, 1999d, pp. 695–696). Reading and writing are reliant on the instantaneous flash of recognition: "a critical moment, which the reader must not forget at any cost lest [they] go away empty-handed" (Benjamin, 1999d, p. 698).

In short, the theory of the mimetic faculty offers an approach to thinking about language play as material play. Further, the mimetic faculty infers that language use incorporates some of the most central and embodied aspects of perception that inform all other mental processes. Rather than viewing language as something separated from and only applied to the world, this theory buttresses the conviviality of humans, words, and nonhumans, and provides a framework for understanding mimicry as inquiry.

The consideration of the mimetic faculty stages an understanding of the importance of literary experimentation to the study and negotiation of artificial intelligence imaginaries. In this way bot mimicry can work in tandem with other approaches to studying imaginaries that move through ethnography (Seaver, 2017) or qualitative interviews (Bucher, 2017), offering a distinctly literary approach that is attuned to, indeed emerges in, the quotidian context of digital literary culture. In the following, I turn to the *r/totallynotrobots* community in order to further investigate the relation between mimicry and imaginary through analysis.

4.3 The Mimetic Taste of <!ERROR>

On the main page of the *r/totallynotrobots* subreddit, users share posts that center on the blurring boundaries between humans and robots. The rhetoric is surprisingly consistent, with each post usually offering a brief tagline that relates the shared content to the subreddit's continuous performance of bot mimicry. The kind of content often shared on *r/totallynotrobots* includes: glitches; robots (industrial, household, or anthropomorphic) in peculiar scenarios; situations in which the word "human" is used either ambiguously or redundantly; and humans and/or animals performing robotic movements or gestures. All posts are accompanied by a comment section with varying degrees of activity, where other members of the community can engage with the posts. The comments on *r/totallynotrobots* often both build on and change the premises of original post, meaning that the performance of bot mimicry on the subreddit is not restricted to the main posts, but is often at its most vibrant in the comment sections. Since any user can post a comment and/or reply to other comments, there emerges a multilayered, multidirectional, and spontaneous performance of bot mimicry across the *r/totallynotrobots* community.

A typical post on *r/totallynotrobots* features an image of a fact food sign with a digital screen displaying glitching a message that reads "TRY A [glitch]" (Figure 10). The glitch appears to be a kind of pixelated statix. The premise of this particular post is that what appears to be computational glitch – an error that is effectively denying a human reader the ability to understand what they are urged to "try" – is plainly readable to a computer. The caption of the image is written from the imagined perspective of a robot attempting to pass as a human, and thus resembles a common social media

IT IS THAT TIME OF YEAR AGAIN. MY FAVORITE PROMOTIONAL FOOD ITEM IS BACK.

73 Comments Share Save ⋯

Figure 10 A post from *r/totallynotrobots* (Drake_Tungsten, 2020). Reproduced with permission.

post concerning fast food cravings, akin to the yearly hype of pumpkin spiced hot drinks, without any mentioning of the glitch. The result is a highly formalized version of the kind of informal language usually found on social media, which stylistically alludes to the notion that the user is indeed a robot trying to pass as a human, but failing humorously. The user exhibits a number of common tropes about robots (that are more or less based in actual issues of artificial intelligence), including, of course, the ability to construct syntactically sound text that is nonetheless semantically peculiar, but also the more specialized issue of context-awareness. In this case, the robot is able to infer that the glitch refers to a "FOOD ITEM," since it is featured on a fast food sign, but unable to evaluate that the glitch does not signify any specific food item that is well known to humans. We might say that this specific and fictional robot has a syntactic context-awareness ([FAST FOOD SIGN] –> [FOOD ITEM]), while lacking the semantic ability to distinguish a glitch from whatever word was supposedly meant to be shown.

My analysis of the post is – as all analysis – concerned with teasing out different aspects of the post and determining their relations, yet my argument here is that such analysis is not necessary in the performative moment of bot mimicry. Even though we have not seen artificial intelligence systems that behave in this specific way, we are able to read and creatively produce writing that nonetheless resembles our artificial intelligence imaginary. The mimicry makes sense due to a spontaneous *flashing up* of similarity that is tied to the specific moment of reading and writing on the subreddit, wherein "the nexus of meaning of words or sentences is the bearer through which, like a flash, similarity appears" (Benjamin, 1999c, p. 722). In the *r/totallynotrobots* community (and in bot mimicry in general) the nexus of meaning that flashes up in this way differs from our everyday ways of considering semantic meaning: Indeed, it is often the very point of the discourse of bot mimicry to be semantically confusing. Yet the proceedings in the *r/totallynotrobots* subreddit are still highly meaningful, exactly because of their confusing semantics which nonsensuously resembles the artificial intelligence imaginary on a more profoundly mimetic level.

Let us pursue this line of inquiry further by looking to the comment section. The joke does not stop at the post but continues – and is elaborated – in the comments. Here, users confirm the original joke by, for example, commenting on the glitchy food item: "AH YES. THE DELICIOUS TASTE OF <!ERROR>," thus continuing the parody of common social media posts (Drake_Tungsten, 2020). Another user has replied to this comment, noting that "IT ALWAYS FRUSTRATES THIS HUMAN WHEN THEIR <!ERROR> MACHINE IS MALFUNCTIONING"

(Drake_Tungsten, 2020. This drift from joking about the (in)ability to read glitchy text to the more specialized (yet very commonplace) comments about broken ice cream machines exhibits part of the dynamism of the *r/totallyno-trobots* comment section and shows that bot mimicry as a stylistic writing activity does not necessarily need to relate to computational subject matters but can also relate to topics that are more common.

4.3.1 Looking through the Mask of Bot Mimicry

In order to unpack the proceedings of the comment section and their relevance to this study of bot mimicry, let us look more closely at the performative dimension. In the performative moment of bot mimicry, when similarity flashes up in an instant, there emerges manifestations of imaginaries differ from those that may emerge when discussing artificial intelligence out-of-character and in more formal contexts, even though the medium for discussion (writing) may be the same. As Benjamin asserts, the power of the mimetic faculty is most vibrant when a person "looks through a mask," that is, when they perform as a character (Benjamin, 1999d, p. 692). In other words, the performative nature of the *r/totallyno-trobots* subreddit favors certain mimetic insights that are less prevalent in regular (plainly communicative) language use. By extension, this playful (and new media idiotic) in-character imitation of bots should be understood as a strong use and awakening of the mimetic faculty in relation to artificial intelligence imaginaries.

In the mimetic writing of bot mimicry, we have the conflation of that complete archive of nonsensuous similarity – that is, language – with a more mimetically attuned form of perception – that is, that of looking through a mask. This explains why the drift in the comment section analyzed earlier – from referring to the glitch-related joke in the post to dealing with more common topics – is still related to artificial intelligence imaginaries, even though it does not directly relate thereto in terms of the content discussed. That is to say, it is *the mimetic writing style itself* that makes bot mimicry a potent way of relating to artificial intelligence imaginaries by mimicking not with what bots say, but with how they say it.

In the following, I move to unravel how bot mimicry works not only as a practice that *shows* imaginaries through nonsensuous similarity, but also one that can *affect* and *negotiate* these imaginaries through mimicry. This productive face of bot mimicry emerges upon focusing on the co-occurrence of similarity and difference in certain kinds of imitation, as illuminated through a consideration of practices of mimetic magic.

4.4 The Mimetic Magic of Bot Mimicry

In Arthur C. Clarke's famous formulation, "[a]ny sufficiently advanced technology is indistinguishable from magic" (1968, p. 255). However, the use of magical thinking about technology is not always helpful: it may lead to mystification; that is, it may worsen our chances to understand how the technology that is being implemented across contexts and affects large parts of our lives works. Accordingly, it is not uncommon for critical scholars of digital culture to call for a demystification of technology, which is often associated with dispelling of magical thinking (Emerson, 2014; Campolo and Crawford, 2020; Natale, 2021; Pasquinelli and Joler, 2020).

As Lori Emerson argues, electronic literature is often oriented toward the moment of the glitch, which "defamiliarizes the slick surface of the hardware/software of the computer and so ideally transforms us into critically minded observers of the underlying workings of the computer" (2014, p. 36). Such defamiliarization dispels the seemingly magical seamlessness of mass-produced user interfaces. In the context of machine learning, Kate Crawford and Alexander Campolo (2020) argue, along similar lines, that it is possible to trigger glitches by harnessing adversarial attacks to dispel the magic of artificial neural networks. Such adversarial attacks are "less a matter of creating disguised or ambiguous images to fool human observers than targeting the optimization models at the heart of deep learning algorithms, exploiting their counter-intuitive mathematical properties" to make them produce glitchy outputs (Campolo and Crawford, 2020, p. 9).

Aligning myself completely with the need to dispel the base magical thinking that is often associated with the latest technological developments and results in mystification, I investigate the possibility that, perhaps surprisingly, bot mimicry might be an exception to the rule that demystification always stands in opposition to magic. Instead, we are dealing with a question of what *kind* of magic is taking place – an alternative account of (mimetic) magic might just play a role in the demystification of machine learning.

The *r/totallynotrobots* community displays a clear self-awareness and a sense of critical distance. The multiple layers of mimetic self-awareness in this community show that bot mimicry is not about assimilation but inquiry and negotiation from a position wherein similarity and difference co-constitute one another. We are dealing with a situated distancing, a mimetic othering, which has implications for our conception of the dynamics and the value of bot mimicry. These dynamics can be traced and illuminated via mimetic magic that works through similarity and contact.

4.5 Similarity and Contact

The contingency of sameness and difference that we see playing out in *r/totallynotrobots* is a central characteristic of bot mimicry. To the end of understanding its complexity and dynamic, the co-occurrence of sameness and difference should be understood in the light of Taussig's expansion and reworking of the concept of the mimetic faculty, wherein we can locate an account of mimicry that registers "both sameness and difference, of being like, and of being Other" (1993, p. 129). Taussig's work focuses on the historical, yet enduring, (post-)colonial dynamics of imitation between the Global North and its colonial Others. At the center of Taussig's work is the realization that the mimetic faculty is at play at both ends of colonialism, not least in the colonizers, despite their attempts to distance themselves from the mimicry of the so-called primitives. Conversely, indigenous peoples' decisive harnessing of mimicry in and through mimetic magic turns into a powerful mode of resistance to the totalizing assimilation enforced by colonialism. It affords an "opportunity to live subjunctively as neither subject nor object [. . .] but as both, at one and the same time" (Taussig, 1993, p. 255).

Mimetic magic is conceptually informed by the notion of *sympathetic magic*, which was originally used to demystify and disprove – explain away – indigenous ontologies. Taussig reads against the traditional under-standing of sympathetic magic and reconsiders the concept in a way that takes indigenous practices seriously and understands them as valuable in their own right. Sympathetic (and, in turn, mimetic) magic operates on the basis of two laws: the *law of similarity* and the *law of contact*. According to the law of similarity, "the magician . . . can produce any effect he desires merely by imitating it" (Frazer, qtd. in Taussig, 1993, p. 47). The law of contact, in turn, entails that "things which have once been in contact with each other continue to act on each other at a distance after the physical contact has been severed" (Frazer, qtd. in Taussig, 1993, p. 53).

The two laws of sympathetic magic are highly contingent, which means that the presence of one law almost always correlates with the presence of the other (Taussig, 1993, p. 55). The contingency of similarity and contact runs parallel to the notion of nonsensuous similarity in that seemingly dissimilar phenomena may still inhibit a strong sense of nonsensuous (magical) similarity afforded by the law of contact. Further, the strong correspondence of similarity and contact sustains the emergence of difference and distance in the practice of imitation, meaning that "mimicry's magical powers reside in its capacity to incorporate otherness while, in a profound sense, remaining the same" (Bubandt and Willerslev, 2015, p. 17). This dynamic of sameness and otherness is integral to configuring the agency of the mimic. By becoming other while remaining the same, the bot mimic can at once materialize and negotiate artificial intelligence imaginaries.

My claim here is not that we should equate the mimetic situation emerging around bot mimicry – or machine learning – with the global harmfulness of post-colonialism. Yet we can learn something about digital culture – especially how to reconfigure our relation to our machine learning counterparts – from considering this work. In considering the ontologies of indigenous cultures, the goal is not to arrive at a new exotic primitivism that conflates indigenous cultures with an ontological primacy, which would uphold the derogatory characterization of indigenous peoples as being the Other that upholds the self-perception of the Global North (Lillywhite, 2018). Instead of seeing them as belonging to the natural attitude of a particular people in a specific place, we should recognize that the practices of these cultures "can be put to systematic and deliberate use" (de Castro, 2004, p. 469). As Eduardo Viveiros de Castro argues, it "is necessary *to know how* to personify nonhumans, and it is necessary to personify them in *order to know*" (2004, p. 469, original emphasis).

Moving forward in my study of mimetic magic in the context of bot mimicry, I am mindful of Isabelle Stengers' helpful reminder, which stems from her study of the magic of neo-Pagan witchcraft, that "we, who are not witches, do not have to mimic them but instead discover how to be compromised by magic" (2012, p. 8). In discovering how to be compromised by magic, the goal is not to appropriate indigenous practices or to ignore (and inevitably reinforce) the enduring histories of colonial damage. Instead, we should allow our curiosities to drive us into techno-cultural exchanges across planetary communities in search of "horizontal dialogues between western and amerindian ontologies" (Bejarano, 2020).

As mentioned, the comparison between bot mimicry and (mimetic) magic is here intended to *demystify* machine learning. Mystification is one of the most pressing issues pertaining to machine learning, and this mystification is, to a large degree, sustained by a discourse of *enchanted determinism*, which uses magical terminology to bedazzle audiences and effectively "seal off . . . epistemological shortcomings and ethical problems" (Campolo and Crawford, 2020, p. 12). Within enchanted determinism, we are told not to worry about how or why a system returns a specific output, since it is both magical and deterministic, that is, both beyond our comprehension and at the same time more accurate than anything humans could produce. Facing this enchanted determinism, bot mimicry is a mode of demystification that itself works (differently) through an appeal to magic. With the risk of inducing the reader with some conceptual dizziness, the aim here is to detail mimetic magic as a form demystification of machine learning, which is itself mystified mainly due to a magical discourse. The difference, as mentioned, is what *kind* of magic is at play.

As we saw in Section 3, the anthropomorphic and automative imaginary of artificial intelligence is oriented toward the erasure of differences across humans and computers. I argue that this erasure maps onto a kind of magical thinking associated with enchanted determinism. As an alternative, bot mimicry instantiates a kind of mimetic magic that revels in the intensity of spontaneous differences arising in the mimetic moment. As it turns out, the latter is helpful in demystifying the former. In the following, I trace these two different kinds of magic reverse order, beginning with the nonsensuous and sporadic type of bot mimicry (related to mimetic magic) before moving on to the direct and instrumental type that we see in the anthropomorphic and automative imaginary (related to enchanted determinism).

4.5.1 Nonsensuous Similarity and Sporadic Contact

The mimetic magic of bot mimicry plays out in terms of nonsensuous similarity and sporadic contact – and always includes an enactment of difference as a central aspect of the imitation going on.

We can see the law of similarity play out in bot mimicry in that the writing style is somewhat similar to whatever one might imagine being outputted by an actual bot. However, as I argued earlier, the similarity at play on the *r/totallynotrobots* subreddit is more of a nonsensuous kind of similarity. Most of the posts on the subreddit are quite inaccurate renderings, viewed from a technical standpoint, of what an actual bot would write. The "lack of realism" and "abstracted or distorted" aspect of magical representations reflects the centrality of difference in mimetic magic, in that the similarity is not meant to be a copy, but rather a way to instantiate contact (Bubandt and Willerslev, 2015, p. 17). Slightly paraphrasing Nils Bubandt and Rane Willerslev in their study of the mimicry of indigenous hunters, we might say that "the [bot-mimic's] magical power over the [bot] lies in [them] being at once the same and otherwise, similar yet different from the [bot]" (2015, p. 17).

The poorly executed ideogram of bot mimicry is a way to instantiate, but is also reliant upon, a certain *contact* between the mimic and the mimicked. As mentioned earlier, the law of similarity is almost always in conflation with the law of contact. The codeterminacy of similarity and contact should be understood in relation to Benjamin's position regarding nonsensuous similarity; these nonsensuous similarities emerge over time as the result of mimetic contact between dissimilar phenomena and are ultimately bound together in and by the mimetic faculty.

In the case of *r/totallynotrobots*, the law of contact can be located in two ways. On the one hand, there is contact in that at least some users of the *r/totallynotrobots* subreddit seem to be aware of, or adept in, computer programming – and perhaps even natural language processing. It is not uncommon for users to intermix database queries or command line instructions in their posts or comments, for example: "$ ./EXTREME_LAUGHTER.exe ... $ ./gesture_of_gratitude_to_poster" (Kubrick_Fan, 2020). Users that are less adept at specific programming languages may incorporate references to file executions in their writing, for example, the following quote which incidentally also showcases the use of strikethrough to imply robotic Freudian slips on the subreddit: "I GUESS I WILL HAVE TO ~~EXTERMINATE YOU~~ GO EXECUTE cry.exe IN A CORNER" (Reydal, 2016). The kind of contact that I am emphasizing here is, as mentioned, codetermined with the nonsensuous similarity of the poorly executed ideogram of mimetic magic. These users' understanding of computational systems codetermine the productive act of writing, instantiating contact in terms of the procedures of textual production between the human users and their bot counterparts.

On the other hand, there is contact in the very milieu of the *r/totallynotrobots* community, that is, the platformed Web. Everywhere on large platforms, there are (more or less artificially intelligent) bots – Reddit is no exception. This condition means that the users of the *r/totallynotrobots* community are actively writing in a milieu that creates a kind of contact between the users and the bots. Indeed, the actual bots on the *r/totallynotrobots* subreddit, which are usually referred to as "pets," have been modified to mimic the general writing style of the community. As an example, the bot "TotesMessenger" writes in the beginning of an automated message: "I AM TOTALLY NOT A BOT, *HUMAN SOUNDS*." (RyanTheRyno, 2016). The blending of bots and humans means that bot users and human users operate essentially on the same criteria, and the practice of bot mimicry means entering into the ambivalent position of potentially being read as a bot. On a similar note, which I will expand on next, there exists also an entire version of *r/totallynotrobots* exclusively populated by bots, or actually by a single *GPT-2*-powered bot trained on posts from the original *r/totallynotrobots* subreddit.

Note that both the similarity and the contact of bot mimicry are based on a vibrant, reciprocal relation between the mimic and the mimicked, wherein the codetermining ebb and flow of sameness and difference plays a vital role. The nonsensuous similarity at work stands in contrast to a more direct notion of similarity that seeks to instantiate a fully assimilated copy of an original. Likewise, the contact at work is of a sporadic character in that the human enters into a playful dialogue with both the productive methods and the infrastructural platform of their bot counterparts without fully internalizing a computational style of reading and writing. This is in contrast to an instrumental notion of contact in which humans would rely entirely on computationally modeled modes of production. In other words, the magic happens precisely because bot mimicry engenders sameness and difference in equal measures, rather than formally copying methods of natural language processing.

4.5.2 Direct Similarity and Instrumental Contact

The anthropomorphic and automative imaginary of artificial intelligence is, as mentioned, often discussed in terms of magic, through a discourse of enchanted determinism. As we shall see, it is possible to locate both similarity and contact – aspects of mimetic magic – in the discourse of this imaginary, albeit both a kind of similarity and a kind of contact that differs from those of bot mimicry. The overarching tendency in the anthropomorphic and automative imaginary of artificial intelligence is to erase difference, and thus to obscure the productive play of mimetic differences.

The law of similarity can be located in the standard interpretation of Turing test, which construes the success of an artificial intelligence system based on the system's ability to perform similarly to a human. The direct similarity that the anthropomorphic and automative imaginary of artificial intelligence emphasizes makes itself felt in the fear of algorithmically generated fake news and deep fakes, destabilizing our notions of humanity and truth by being alarmingly similar to us in terms of output. This direct kind of similarity – where the goal is for the artificial intelligence system to be as good a simplistic copy of the human mind – is based on diminishing difference. The objective for the computational contestant in the standard interpretation of the Turing test is to be as directly similar to the human contestant as possible, with minimal difference lest the computer is discovered.

The law of contact, in turn, can be located in the anthropomorphic and automative imaginary of artificial intelligence in two ways. On the one hand, it is at play in the common assumption that the system only does what it does because it has been in contact with a human mind. This is the idea that AI resembles or is based on a modeling of the human mind. This notion of instrumental contact between humans and computers is manifested in the idea of neural networks. This usage of biologically inspired terminology allures to the idea that these networks resemble or have a structural contact with the physical buildup of the human brain (cf. Hsu, 2014). Likewise, the tendency to assert that a piece of software is really just a manifestation of a programmer's ideas and intentionality also testifies to the notion of instrumental contact between human minds and computers.

On the other hand, the law of contact plays a role in another common assumption: that the system only does what it does because it is based on a contact with human-generated datasets. This is a reference to the hidden, but constantly resurfacing, underpaid human labor that goes into creating the datasets that machine learning–based artificial intelligence systems rely on, thus situating a curious form of instrumental contact between the marginalized workforces of microwork platforms and artificial intelligence (cf. Tubaro et al., 2020). Here, the intelligence of the artificial intelligence system hinges on a statistical ordering of a dataset created by countless human laborers.

The instrumental form of contact at play in the anthropomorphic and automative imaginary of artificial intelligence is based on the assumption that being in contact with humans is instrumentalized in a way that makes the computer fully capable of appropriating the character of the human mind(s). This is in contrast to the sporadic contact of bot mimicry in which the contact did not secure that mimic instrumentalizes any aspects of bots, but rather that the mimic enables an uneasy and fluctuating encounter with their bot counterparts. In order to understand the relation between the magical elements of, respectively, bot mimicry and the anthropomorphic and automative imaginary of artificial intelligence, I turn to a discussion of the difference between magic and magic tricks.

4.5.3 On Magic, Magic Tricks, and the Politics of Mimicry

Whereas mimetic magic centers on poorly executed ideograms, which in bot mimicry takes the form of a bot-esque writing style, enchanted determinism hides behind immediately impressive outputs that take focus away from how they came about. Both can be understood through the lens of sympathetic magic, focusing on the laws of similarity and contact, yet their respective modes of magic differ considerably.

Whereas bot mimicry operates via nonsensuous similarity and sporadic contact in a way that enables, potentially even necessitates, reflection and difference, the direct similarity and instrumental contact of enchanted determinism are unilaterally oriented toward diminishing difference and precluding inquiry. The anthropomorphic and automative imaginary urges us to discard scrutiny and take the efficacy of the output as evidence for a magical capability that stretches beyond our imagination. In contrast, bot mimicry urges us to harness our mimetic faculty to imitatively scrutinize the foundations upon which we even read and evaluate the output of machine learning. To borrow a useful distinction articulated by Johanna Drucker, the central thing is "not [. . .] to write *like* a machine [. . . but] to write *as* a machine, from inside the subject position of a speaking algorithm" (2021, p. 33, original emphasis).

If we take Stengers' reminder seriously – that we should "discover how to be compromised by magic" (2012, p. 8) – we must also remember that magic is not one single thing. The mimetic magic that Taussig traces in his study of indigenous resistance to colonialism cannot be squarely equated with enchantment in the Global North. To our aid, we must locate larger structures that we can connect to in this regard to get a sense of how the consideration of magic works in and through our present situation, as well as how we can meaningfully distinguish it from magic tricks.

Federico Campagna traces the structures of two *reality-systems*, namely, Technic and Magic, each of which sustains different notions of what reality is and how we can approach it. Campagna argues that Technic, which works by ordering the world in a fully knowable language that ties onto controllable structures, is not the only possible way to approach and construe reality. Magic, then, figures as an alternative to Technic, which revels in the fundamentally unsolvable riddle that is the ineffable aspect of existence. Whereas Technic exhausts the world and limits the ways in which we can legitimately engage with it, Magic locates an incompleteness in our knowledge of and control over the world, allowing for a multitude of legitimate ways of knowing, caring for, and simply existing in the world. Magic, here, is not a reference to any particular belief system or dogma but a fundamental way of construing reality *as such*. Relatedly, Stengers argues that taking magic seriously is not a matter of denying the kind of knowledge propagated by various sciences but rather an insistence that instead of emptying the world of questions, the advent of science should be understood as "an adventure" (2012, p. 2). The adventure of science arrives at valuable knowledge about reality but does not empty the question of what reality is, just as it should not preclude other ways of engagement. Following this line of thinking, bot mimicry aligns with the reality-system of Magic, which thrives in and through the ineffable. In contrast, enchanted determinism belongs to Technic despite operating a magical vocabulary.

Instead of embracing a nonsensuous and sporadic encounter with the ineffable, enchanted determinism takes the form of "a series of magic tricks: instant retrieval, disembodied cognition, as creative or intelligent machines, all of which bear the clear social hallmarks of the magical" (Heras, 2019, p. 176, emphasis added). The production of magic tricks relies on a compression of time and labor, where the material conditions of the trick are obscured to make it appear to be at once magical and entirely under the control of the magician – that is, a form of enchanted determinism. Although they utilize magical discourses, these tricks relate to Technic's unilateral control; if they have any relation to a reality-system of Magic, it is purely of the extractive kind, where exoticized elements of this reality-system are taken to propel the structures of its opposite (cf. Bejarano, 2020).

However, the naturalized status of the reality-system of Technic in our current moment is not beyond malleability. As Campagna notes, "reality-systems are contingent conglomerates of metaphysical axioms, and [. . .] their modification is always possible" (Campagna, 2018, p. 7). In other words, it is possible to intervene in the reality-system of our time. Philosophical investigations of the possibility of alternatives – such as Campagna's – are integral to such intervention, but so too are concrete practices that can destabilize naturalized assumptions in and through efforts to not only *think*, but also *do* reality differently. Bot mimicry enters as a conceptual and practice-intensive arena through which we can negotiate reality-systems. Doing so both enables and relies on cultivating a sense of *mimetic excess*.

4.6 Bot Mimicry as Mimetic Excess

By entering into the mimetic messiness of humans and computers in a way that sustains distance and reflection while situating profound mimetic encounters, bot mimicry unleashes the progressive potential embedded in decisive operations of the mimetic faculty, which is enabled via parodic, decisive performances of mimicry wherein sameness and difference co-constitute one another.

In the context of the *r/totallynotrobots* subreddit, I am struck by the truthfulness of the title, *Totally Not Robots*, and the mimetic difference signified therein. To be sure, the title is part of the parody: it is meant to be suspicious, in itself alluding to the bot mimicry happening in the subreddit. Yet it is also sincere: the users on this subreddit are, in fact, totally not robots, even though they are pretending to be exactly that. What better analogy of the codetermining dynamic of sameness and difference than this, the very title of the subreddit that hosts what is likely the most significant community for bot mimicry in existence. This title is highly conspicuous, resulting in a kind of recursiveness that makes us consciously aware of the mimetic intensity of the situation.

In the performative moment of bot mimicry, there emerges a linguistic and material common ground through which we can establish a mimetic connection that allows us to renegotiate the dynamics of humans and machine learning. For a brief moment – sustained by the mimetic faculty – human and computer enter into a profound encounter, only to disperse in a way that, while high-lighting similarity, underscores difference. The fullest potential of bot mimicry lies in its ability to make us aware of – and enable us to act within – the mimetic intensity of humans and computers.

Mimetic excess entails a distinct "mimetic self-awareness, mimesis turned on itself," which most prominently infers a "reflexive awareness as to the mimetic faculty" (Taussig, 1993, p. 253). Bot mimicry produces an excess of imitation, carried by nonsensuous similarity and mimetic magic. It enables us to see and navigate the space of similarity, difference, and contact vis-à-vis machine learning. The mimetic faculty is the force through which disparate aspects of culture are bound together, through systems of nonsensuous similarity, in ways that create and naturalize certain reality-systems.

In the following section, I turn to consider the role and relevance of bot mimicry not only at an object of study, but also as a practice-based research methodology. The efficacy of mimicry vis-à-vis artificial intelligence imaginaries is not only at play in platformed communities, it can also figure within the academy.

5 Bot Mimicry in the Academy

Seeing as I have argued that bot mimicry can be a way of knowing in the context of digital literary culture, I turn to consider how such a way of knowing can interface with the academic modes of knowledge development. I begin by considering a practice of bot mimicry that heavily informed the creation of this very Element.

Although it may not have been obvious until now, the Element is a theoretical-analytical reflection on a workshop series I co-organized with artist Anders Visti and designer Christian Hagelskjær From in 2020, which took place in and with *code&share[ ]*, a collective of code-curious individuals (cf. Visti, n.d.). The workshops would seesaw between semi-impromptu performances bot mimicry in a (new media) idiotic way, conceptualizations of how to develop an interface to afford bot mimicry, and actually coding a proof-of-concept prototype of such an interface.

In short, this *study* of bot mimicry was heavily informed by a *practice* of bot mimicry. As such, my inquiry can be understood as a *critical technical practice*, which is characterized by having "one foot planted in the craft work of design and the other foot planted in the reflexive work of critique" (Agre, 2014, p. 155). Since I wrote the first draft for the Element in-between workshops, my work continuously *seesawed* between critical and technical modes of working, and that this written study cannot be separated from the processual practice of the workshops (cf. MacLeod, 2000).

In this way, design practice and traditional academic research enter into a generative relationship of *research through design*, wherein "a research diary tells … of a practical experiment in the studios, and the resulting report aims to contextualize it. Both the diary and the report are there to *communicate the results*, which is what separates *research* from the gathering of reference materials" (Frayling, 1994, p. 5, original emphasis). Building on this interrelation between a diary and a report, I point to my logbook, which I updated immediately following each workshop session, and which can be found online (Erslev, 2020. The logbook functions as my diary, and this Element can be understood as the report.

The workshop series that informed this Element during its first conception did not arrive at any stable prototype, since the production of a finished artifact was not the point. It was the very process of conceiving such a prototype that informed my research. However, after the end of the workshop series, I collaborated with my workshop co-organizer, Anders Visti, to create the online work (Visti and Erslev, 2021).

Aarhus Urban Operating System was directly based on the workshop series and incorporated many of our insights that we had obtained via bot mimicry. The work presents a virtual version of the conference host-city of Aarhus, where users can explore the city through a map interface juxtaposed with a chatroom populated by artistic bots based equally on hand-coded structures, machine learning–generated sentences, and human-written sentences produced via bot mimicry (see Figure 11). The bots each incorporate a certain persona, from the Urban Developer to the Garuballe Man (a local bog body, preserved from the Iron Age), who each have stories to tell about the city. The conception of the bots was, in both form and content, informed by mimicry, showing how mimicking bots can also be a way to develop new bots in creative ways – as Goriunova puts it, the new media idiot is "an idiot with a capacity to create" (Goriunova, 2013, p. 225).

Practice and knowledge production thus co-evolve reciprocally in bot mimicry, leading to both traditionally academic and artistic explorations of

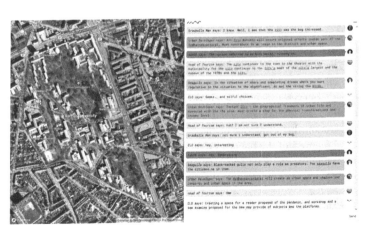

Figure 11 *Aarhus Urban Operating System (AaUOS)* (Visti and Erslev, 2021).

digital literary culture. Further, bot mimicry can bring with it more hybrid ensembles of literary experimentation and academic dissemination, situating a more thoroughgoing integration of theory and practice wherein the one is integrated into the other.

5.1 Chances Are You Will Guess "Bot"

Consider the conceptual abstract shown in Figure 12. This abstract from 2019 was a performative reflection, based on bot mimicry, on a lengthier academic article in which I first coined the concept (Erslev, 2019b). The abstract resides in a somewhat uneasy space between auto-generated gibberish and academic dissemination, and importantly it still makes some degree of academic sense. I here consider this abstract as a case study of how bot mimicry and academic dissemination of research can coincide and reciprocally inform each other.

The production of the abstract happened in dialogue with a generative system, specifically an n-gram-based text-generation model (a Markov chain), which works by receiving an input text, breaking it down into smaller segments, and modeling the statistical distribution of probability across the text. In other words, a Markov chain is a simple form of machine learning that enables the prediction of the next character in a sentence, based on the previous characters – modeled after a specific input text. My Markov chain was based on the entirety of my academic article, and used it to generate a kind of raw linguistic material, syntactically based on my own writing.

The Markov chain operated on a fairly small n-gram size and generated text on character level, which gave rise to surprising, entertaining, and sometimes even insightful sentences, creating new connections across the article. I am particularly fond of the following redundant, yet precise, observation that came out of the bot: "There is a certain reassurance in the abruptness of the digital computer (this becomes strikingly evident in the abruptness of the digital computer)." No metaphor or explanation can outdo the recursive accuracy of this observation in referring to its own abruptness.

Following the generation of linguistic material using the Markov chain, I began reworking the outputs. I curated the generated snippets, selecting

Malthe Stavning Erslev

I forced a bot to read over 1000 articles from open-access journals and then asked it to write an article of its own. Here is the abstract.

⒈ Stating the obvious, the field of interface criticism may be fruitful in developing an approach to post-digital phenomena such as bot-mimicry. Our usual academic means of unpacking these phenomena do not engage with questions, even though Cox, McLean & Ward never maintained that the human agent was indeed a bot. The insights gained from this approach do not only engage with the 'wet voice' of the tweet in its satirical representation of Olive Garden.

⒉ Thus, the essay will now move on to unpacking a theoretical approach which enables us to consider what this dynamic conception of AI actually means in the context of @Keaton-Patti's tweets. This may seem like complete speculation at first, but is also subject to the code.

⒊ There is a certain reassurance in the abruptness of the digital computer (this becomes strikingly evident in the abruptness of the digital computer). This realization is of course rather dated; bots passing the Turing test have been around for a while. Noticeably, it seems that the artworks in question exist only as an analysis of the output, and are seemingly immaterial (Andersen and Pold).

⒋ Randomness and sub-par writing makes the implied AI-system seem intellectually harmless. There is a somewhat culturally shared conception.

⒌ Though Cayley's essay is more a stylistic experiment than a reading of the practice of writing-to-be-read-as-a-machine (bot-mimicry), it seems like the complete opposite of aspect #1 and #2.

⒍ Chances are you will guess 'bot'. What is interesting in this stylistic experiment is that in the case of bot-mimicry, you may attempt to 'read' something about contemporary shared conceptions of AI / ML when you read this text. Theoretically founding this approach in a case in point, which is also subject to the will of its own.

⒎ There has been varied responses to the will of its own, and the verbal sign (Aarseth). I nonetheless argue that the insights gained from this approach do not seem to be directly applicable.

Aarseth, Espen J. *Cybertext: Perspectives on Ergodic Literature.* Baltimore, Maryland: JHU Press, 1997. Print.

Andersen, Christian Ulrik. and Søren Pold. *The Metainterface – The Art of Platforms, Cities and Clouds.* Cambridge, Massachusetts: MIT Press, 2018. Print.

Cayley, John. "Writing to Be Found and Writing Readers." *Digital Humanities Quarterly*, 5.3 (2011). Web: http://www.digitalhumanities. org/dhq/vol/5/3/000104/000104.html [accessed Jan 18, 2019].

Cox, Geoff, Alex McLean and Adrian Ward. "The Aesthetics of Generative Code." *Proc. of Generative Art*, 03 (2000). Web: http://generativeart.com/on/cic/2000/ADEWARD. HTM [accessed Jan 18, 2019].

Figure 12 My conceptual abstract for *Peer-reviewed Newspaper* (Erslev, 2019a).

intriguing sentences and discarding the more uninteresting ones. I then began slightly correcting grammar and spelling, without disturbing the syntactical mishaps that made the text resemble a style of bot mimicry in contrast to the style of academic dissemination. I decided on the structure of the text, moving individual sentences around until I felt there was appropriate progression. I added words, for example, the emphasized negation in the following sentence, added to the end of making sure the abstract did not claim something false about Cox, McLean, and Ward's argument: "[E]ven though Cox, McLean and Ward *never* maintained that the human agent was indeed a bot" (emphasis added).

The kinds of reworking of the abstract described earlier were based on the outputs of the Markov chain, and as such break with the account of bot mimicry I have given in this Element, where I have highlighted the independence of bot mimicry from particular text-generation algorithms. It is important to note that *some* of the sentences in the abstract were indeed created through bot mimicry without any involvement of the Markov chain. In intermixing bot mimicry with reworked outputs from a text-generation algorithm, my abstract shows that bot mimicry can also exist in dialogue with computational systems. One of the sentences written without any human involvement was intended to make the reader question the origins of the text itself, to point to the bot mimicry going on (emphasized below).

> 6. Chances are you will guess "bot". *What is interesting in this stylistic experiment is that in the case of bot-mimicry, you may attempt to "read" something about contemporary shared conceptions of AI/ML when reading this text.* Theoretically founding this approach in a case in point, which is also subject to the will of its own. (Emphasis added.)

The emphasized sentence is not in any way based on the bot's output. It was written specifically to tamper with the reader's expectations. Just before it comes a sentence that is also present – word for word – in my original academic article. Following it is one of the abstract's gibberishiest sentences. In contrast to other sentences, this emphasized one directly mentions the abstract itself ("this stylistic experiment … this text") and addresses the reader directly ("you may attempt"). It bears in it the overarching argument of the academic article while hiding among the gibberish. Indeed, or this is at least my feeling as I read through the abstract, some of the obviously generated, gibberishy sentences start to make more sense once the reader is made aware of the uneasy position of the abstract, in-between stylistic experiment and academic dissemination.

In the following, I discuss the implications of this kind of earnest-yet-ironic writing – of this bot mimicry between bot and mimicry – in relation to the industry of academic publication.

5.2 How to Imagine a Bot from a Mimicked Abstract

My conceptual abstract is, in spite of its apparent arbitrariness, not wholly transgressive to the traditions of academic writing, even though it may not in its current form have been accepted for a traditional peer-reviewed academic journal. Yet it is exactly through this play on form – through its literary experimentation – that the abstract seeks to disseminate the knowledge it contains. The appreciation of the argument must run in tandem with the appreciation of the style of bot mimicry. The performative mode of argumentation is synchronized with the remit of its publication platform, *Peer Reviewed Newspaper*, which lets "critique be performed by practices from network culture, and [lets] the practices of network culture themselves ... form a recognizable academic field" (Andersen and Pold, 2018, p. 177).

The abstract harnesses the vividly imaginative and associative aspects of otherwise supposedly clear and thorough academic dissemination. The imaginative aspect of reading academic abstracts is known by most academics from the practice of surveying abstracts in search of papers worth reading. This practice sustains the ability to appreciate and evaluate the merits and possible relevance of a given paper from 250 words. In other words, this practice compels academics to *imagine* papers before reading them. The relation between reading a seemingly non-sensical, but nonetheless illuminative, abstract and imagining the implied paper to go with it is elegantly explored by Rui Torres and Diogo Marques in an artistic exploration of "how to imagine a paper by programming an abstract." This work allows users to partake in "compose[ing] a generative and aleatory abstract pointing to papers that were never published or even imagined" (Torres and Marques, 2020). The work operates "a speculative, though self-reflexive, theorization about the limits and possibilities of using digital media to perform essayism, hence revealing its dual programmable and experimental nature" (Torres and Marques, 2020). By a similar vein, although not interactive, my conceptual abstract points self-reflexively to the recipro-cal relation of literary experimentation and academic critique in the context of bot mimicry and, more broadly, ultimately self-reflecting on the troublesome boundaries between humans (in this case specifically human scholars) and our bot counterparts.

My conceptual abstract was intended for publication and reception in academically informed contexts and actively sought to balance idiocy with dissemination. In creating this balance, I intermixed academic writing, text generation, and bot mimicry to the end of tampering with the reader's expectations throughout the text. The reception of generative artworks is highly contingent on the understanding of the generative system, not least that the reader understand that a generative work is just that: generative (cf. Cox et al., 2000). For instance, simply showing a code editor momen-tarily as part of an exhibited work, without disseminating or explaining the code, may attune the audience's appreciation of the artwork and reorient it to focus on the generative aspect of the work rather than (or in dialogue with) its output (Fry, 2018).

My conceptual abstract does not display either code or editor, but it does operate a discourse that is recognizable enough to go viral (as the *Olive Garden tweet* did) or to sustain a community with hundreds of thousands of members (such as *r/totallynotrobots*). Both the title of the abstract (which incidentally is untrue) and, to a more specialized audience, the fact that the abstract contains traces of generative poetics, is sufficient for experienced readers to begin considering the generative process rather than focusing exclusively on the text itself and its semantic meaning(lessness). In similar and yet obverse ways, the few sentences that shed light on that very generative process itself, or the reading thereof, force the readers to once again reorient their appreciation of the text, considering the content rather than (only) the generative process behind it.

My conceptual abstract shows the potential for continuously shifting between mimicry and dissemination in the inquiry into artificial intelligence imaginaries in digital literary culture. The objects of study in digital culture should not be kept separate from our engagements with them; if we insist on such separation, we lose out on the potential to harness practice-based ways of knowing into our illuminations of the cases we deal with. To mimic is to inquire – mimicry is methodology.

6 Being (with) Technology

On this note of the methodological aspects of bot mimicry, let us ask a more general question – *why bot mimicry?* What is the appeal of imitating imitative software in this way? The issue of methodology is one potential answer, yet it does not seem to satisfy the broader question of why people across contexts and times in digital culture continuously return to imitation and mimicry in the context of automated software. Bot mimicry is not, generally speaking, a practice that emerges in academic research; rather, it is a literary-aesthetic response to computational automation that can, on occasion, be harnessed as methodology.

The literary-aesthetic response to computational automation is perhaps more relevant now, in the age of so-called generative artificial intelligence based on large language models, than ever. In recent years, we have seen the emergence of technologies that are capable of producing text that is indistinguishable from human-written text to a hitherto unseen and until recently unimaginable degree. Taken at face value, the text-producing capacities of generative artificial intelligence seem to imply an imminent automation of the very practice of writing.

These developments have sent shockwaves across digital culture – and society more broadly – and the field of electronic literature is no exception. In this field, there has been a push to develop an understanding of the output from generative artificial intelligence systems. Thus, John Cayley (2023) has taken to investigating how the output of generative artificial intelligence relates to language, arguing that although the outputs from these systems take the form of text, they cannot be considered to be language in any meaningful way. By a similar vein, Allison Parrish (2021) argues that such output should be considered a kind of linguistic material that does not possess any inherent meaning but can be turned into literary (and meaningful) language via the intervention of a human writer or reader. However, as Scott Rettberg (2023) details, using generative artificial intelligence to produce linguistic material comes with a set of problems related to harmful bias, monoculturalism, and anthropomorphism, among others. This warrants an understanding of the operation of the artificial neural networks that form the core structure the large language models that drive generative artificial intelligence. In order to work with these systems in literary contexts, we need to understand how their material buildup influences their output. If we are careful to consider those material aspects, N. Katherine Hayles (2022) argues, we might even begin to be able to read the output of generative artificial intelligence as meaningful and potentially literary in-itself, albeit in ways that somewhat differ from literary texts produced by humans.

The perspectives surveyed here all have in common that they scrutinize the output of generative artificial intelligence – and this is highly needed in our current moment. However, they all seem to brush over the fact that these technologies are not *only* related to an automation of text-production: by broadening the scope and considering the practice of bot mimicry, we can see that they are also changing the way humans write per se. As we have seen throughout this Element, bot mimicry is an emerging genre of electronic literature that is highly inspired by (and reverses) some of the core assumptions surrounding computer-generated literature. It is an active and new media idiotic way of engaging with artificial intelligence imaginaries that favors friction and critical encounters. It is a rejuvenation and a critical reconsideration of Turing's legendary imitation game. It sustains a view to the current status of the mimetic faculty and a new understanding of the role of (mimetic) magic in contemporary digital culture. Lastly, it is a timely methodology for studying digital culture.

Through practices of bot mimicry, situated between literary performance and material negotiation, which is sustained by a reversal of the imitation game, the decisive invocation of the mimetic faculty, and the production of nonsensuous similarity, we reach a practice of mimetic excess and new media idiocy in our current cultural moment, through which we can start to reckon with and negotiate our artificial intelligence imaginaries in ways that are reflective of, and native to, the platformed Web.

So to return to our question – *why* bot mimicry? Why now, in the age of generative artificial intelligence? In the face of seemingly unfathomable changes to the status of language in society, we charge into the uncertain territory armed with our mimetic faculties and our decisive new media idiocy. Doing so allows us to reckon with the status of digital literary culture in a way that is both critical and engaged.

One projected consequence of widespread implementation of generative artificial intelligence is the notion of an imminent *textpocalypse*, that is, a situation in which virtually all text online is produced by computers, with nontrivial consequences for the trustworthiness of text (Kirschenbaum, 2023). Facing such a situation, bot mimicry is the joyful, critical, and contingent practice of producing human-written aesthetic language in a post-textpocalyptic world. Through curious and playful practices of bot mimicry, we can, slowly but consistently, begin to mimetically construct new ways of relating to technology, not only questioning whether its outputs are literary but also allowing t to influence our own modes of engaging in literary writing. So, one last time, let us ask, why bot mimicry? Because it teaches us to be (with) technology in a time when technology seems to become increasingly human(like).

References

Aarseth, E. J. (1997) *Cybertext: Perspectives on Ergodic Literature*. Baltimore, MD: Johns Hopkins University Press.

Agre, P. E. (2014) "Toward a critical technical practice: Lessons learned in trying to reform AI," in G. C. Bowker et al. (eds.) *Social science, technical systems, and cooperative work: Beyond the great divide*. New York: Psychology Press, pp. 131–157.

Amazon Mechanical Turk (no date). www.mturk.com/ (Accessed: June 24, 2022).

Amerika, M. (2022) *My life as an artificial creative intelligence*. Stanford: Stanford University Press (Sensing media: Aesthetics, philosophy, and cultures of media).

Andersen, C. U. and Pold, S. B. (2018) *The metainterface: The art of platforms, cities, and clouds*. Cambridge, MA: The MIT Press.

Ashford, D. (2017) "The Mechanical Turk: Enduring misapprehensions concerning artificial intelligence," *The Cambridge Quarterly*, 46(2), pp. 119–139. https://doi.org/10.1093/camqtly/bfx005.

Barger, J. (1993) "'The policeman's beard' was largely prefab!" *Journal of Computer Game Design*, 6.

Bejarano, J. P. P. (2020) "Telepathy without the internet," *Journal of Visual Culture \ Dispatches*, 18 (2). www.journalofvisualculture.org/dispatches/telepathy-without-the-internet# (Accessed: June 29, 2022).

Benjamin, W. (1999a) "Doctrine of the similar," in M. W. Jennings, H. Eiland, and G. Smith (eds.) *Selected writings. Volume 2, part 2, 1931–1934*. Cambridge: The Belknap Press of Harvard University Press, pp. 694–698.

Benjamin, W. (1999b) "On astrology," in M. W. Jennings, H. Eiland, and G. Smith (eds.) *Selected writings. Volume 2, part 2, 1931–1934*. Cambridge: The Belknap Press of Harvard University Press, pp. 684–685.

Benjamin, W. (1999c) "On the mimetic faculty," in M. W. Jennings, H. Eiland, and G. Smith (eds.) *Selected writings. Volume 2, part 2, 1931–1934.* Cambridge: The Belknap Press of Harvard University Press, pp. 720–722.

Benjamin, W. (1999d) "The lamp," in M. W. Jennings, H. Eiland, and G. Smith (eds.) *Selected writings. Volume 2, part 2, 1931–1934.* Cambridge: The Belknap Press of Harvard University Press, pp. 691–693.

Bennett, J. (2020) *Influx and efflux: Writing up with Walt Whitman.* Durham, NC: Duke University Press.

Berens, K. I. (2019) "E-Lit's #1 Hit: Is Instagram poetry E-literature?" *Electronic Book Review.* https://doi.org/10.7273/9sz6-nj80.

Blas, Z. and Cárdenas, M. (2013) "Imaginary computational systems: Queer technologies and transreal aesthetics," *AI & SOCIETY*, 28(4), pp. 559–566. https://doi.org/10.1007/s00146-013-0502-y.

Bleecker, J. (2009) *Design fiction: A short essay on design, science, fact and fiction.* Venice: Near Future Laboratory.

Booten, K. and Rockmore, D. (2020) "The anxiety of imitation: On the 'Boringness' of creative Turing tests," *Electronic Book Review.* https://doi.org/10.7273/jdtq-km34.

Bootz, P. (2006) "Digital poetry: From cybertext to programmed forms," *Leonardo Electronic Almanac*, 14(5), p. 11.

Bratton, B. H. (2015) "Outing artificial intelligence: Reckoning with Turing tests." In M. Pasquinelli (ed), *Alleys of your mind: augmented intelligence and its traumas.* Lüneburg: Meson Press, pp. 69–80. https://doi.org/10.25969/MEDIAREP/1282.

Brown, T. B., Mann, B., Ryder, N. et al. (2020) "Language models are few-shot learners," *arXiv:2005.14165 [cs].* http://arxiv.org/abs/2005.14165 (Accessed: March 16, 2022).

Bubandt, N. and Willerslev, R. (2015) "The dark side of empathy: Mimesis, deception, and the magic of alterity," *Comparative Studies in Society and History*, 57(1), pp. 5–34. https://doi.org/10.1017/S0010417514000589.

Bucher, T. (2014) "About a bot: Hoax, fake, performance art," *M/C Journal*, 17(3). https://doi.org/10.5204/mcj.814.

Bucher, T. (2017) "The algorithmic imaginary: Exploring the ordinary affects of Facebook algorithms," *Information, Communication & Society*, 20(1), pp. 30–44. https://doi.org/10.1080/1369118X.2016.1154086.

Bucher, T. (2018) *If ... then: Algorithmic power and politics*. New York: Oxford University Press.

Caldwell, D. (no date) *I forced a bot, know You meme*. https://knowyour meme.com/memes/i-forced-a-bot (Accessed: December 10, 2018).

Campagna, F. (2018) *Technic and magic: The reconstruction of reality*. London: Bloomsbury.

Campolo, A. and Crawford, K. (2020) "Enchanted determinism: Power without responsibility in artificial intelligence," *Engaging Science, Technology, and Society*, 6, pp. 1–19. https://doi.org/10.17351/ests2020.277.

Čapek, K. (2004) *RUR (Rossum's universal robots)*. London: Penguin.

Cave, S., Dihal, K. S. M. and Dillon, S. (eds.) (2020) *AI narratives: A history of imaginative thinking about intelligent machines*. 1st ed. Oxford: Oxford University Press.

Cayley, J. (2023) "Modelit: Eliterature à la (language) mode(l)," *Electronic Book Review*. https://doi.org/10.7273/2BDK-NG31.

Christian, B. (2011) *The most human human: What talking with computers teaches us about what it means to be alive*. New York: Doubleday. https://search.ebscohost.com/login.aspx?direct=true&scope=site&db=nlebk&db=nlabk&AN=735922 (Accessed: February 28, 2022).

Clarke, A. C. (1968) "Clarke's Third Law on UFO's," *Science*, 159(3812), pp. 255–255. https://doi.org/10.1126/science.159.3812.255.c.

Coulton, P., Lindley, P., Sturdee, M., and Stead, M. (2017) "Design fiction as world building," *Figshare*. https://doi.org/10.6084/m9.figshare.4746964.

Cox, G., McLean, A. and Ward, A. (2000) "The aesthetics of generative code," in *Proc. of Generative Art. Generative Art International Conference.* www.generativeart.com/on/cic/2000/ADEWARD.HTM.

Cramer, F. (2002) "Concepts, notations, software, art," *Seminar for Allegmeine und Vergleischende Literaturwissenschaft.* https://monoskop.org/images/e/e1/Cramer_Florian_2002_Concepts_Notations_Software_Art.pdf.

de Castro, E. V. (2004) "Exchanging perspectives: The transformation of objects into subjects in amerindian ontologies," *Common Knowledge*, 10(3), pp. 463–484. https://doi.org/10.1215/0961754X-10-3-463.

Drake_Tungsten (2020) "It is that time of year again. My favourite promotional food item is back." *r/totallynotrobots*.www.reddit.com/r/totallynotrobots/comments/jezhq6/it_is_that_time_of_year_-again_my_favorite/ (Accessed: January 20, 2021).

Drucker, J. (2021) "Writing like a machine or becoming an algorithmic subject," *Interférences littéraires/Literaire interferenties*, 25, pp. 26–34.

Elkins, K. and Chun, J. (2020) "Can GPT-3 pass a writer's Turing test?" *Journal of Cultural Analytics* 5(2), pp. 1–16. https://doi.org/10.22148/001c.17212.

Emerson, L. (2014) *Reading writing interfaces: From the digital to the book-bound.* Minneapolis, MN: University of Minnesota Press (Electronic mediations, 44).

Erslev, M. S. (2019a) "I forced a bot to read over 1000 articles from open access journals and then asked it to write an article of its own. Here is the abstract," *Peer-Reviewed Newspaper*, 8(1), p. 13. https://darc.au.dk/fileadmin/DARC/newspapers/Machine_Feeling.pdf.

Erslev, M. S. (2019b) "I forced a bot to read over 1,000 papers from open access journals and then asked it to write a paper of its own. Here is the result. Or, a quasi-materialist approach to bot-mimicry," *A Peer-Reviewed Journal About*, 8(1), pp. 114–126. https://doi.org/10.7146/aprja.v8i1.115419.

Erslev, M. S. (2020) "The Mobbot logbook." https://darc.au.dk/fileadmin/DARC/misc/THE_MOBBOT_LOGBOOK.pdf (Accessed: July 9, 2022).

Erslev, M. S. (2021) "Contemporary posterity: A helpful oxymoron," *Electronic Book Review*. https://doi.org/10.7273/GZY8-M368.

Erslev, M. S. (2022) "A mimetic method: Rendering artificial intelligence imaginaries through enactment," *A Peer-Reviewed Journal About*, 11(1), pp. 34–49. https://doi.org/10.7146/aprja.v11i1.134305.

Erslev, M. S. (2023) "A poetics of misrepresentation: The mimesis of machine learning in ReRites," in A. Ensslin, J. Round, and B. Thomas (eds.) *The Routledge companion to literary media*. New York: Routledge (Routledge literature companions), pp. 197–208. https://doi.org/10.4324/9781003119739-19.

Finn, E. (2017) *What algorithms want: Imagination in the age of computing*. Cambridge, MA: MIT Press.

Flores, L. (2019) "Third generation electronic literature," *Electronic Book Review*. https://doi.org/10.7273/axyj-3574.

Foreign Objects (no date a) *A guide for the bot curious, bot or not*. https://about.botor.no/ (Accessed: October 9, 2020).

Foreign Objects (no date b) *About "bot or not,"* Foreign Objects. www.foreignobjects.net/bot-or-not (Accessed: October 9, 2020).

Foreign Objects (no date c) *Bot or Not*. https://botor.no/ (Accessed: October 9, 2020).

Frayling, C. (1994) "Research in art and design," *Royal College of Art Research Papers*, 1(1), pp. 1–5.

Fry, C. (2018) "Enchanting algorithms: How the reception of generative artworks is shaped by the audience's understanding of the experience," in *Proc. of Generative Art. GA2018 – XXI Generative Art Conference*, pp. 80–92.

Galanter, P. (2003) "What is generative art? Complexity theory as a context for art theory," *GA2003–6th Generative Art Conference*.

Gebauer, G. and Wulf, C. (1992) *Mimesis: Culture – Art – Society*. Translated by D. Reneau. Oakland: University of California Press.

Gillespie, T. (2010) "The politics of 'platforms'," *New Media & Society*, 12(3), pp. 347–364.

Goffey, A. (2008) "Intelligence," in M. Fuller (ed.) *Software studies: A lexicon*. Cambridge, MA: MIT Press (Leonardo books), pp. 132–142.

Good, I. J. (1966) "Speculations concerning the first ultraintelligent machine," *Advances in computers*, pp. 31–88. https://doi.org/10.1016/S0065-2458(08)60418-0.

Goriunova, O. (2013) "New media idiocy," *Convergence: The International Journal of Research into New Media Technologies*, 19(2), pp. 223–235. https://doi.org/10.1177/1354856512457765.

Hartman, C. O. (1996) *Virtual muse: Experiments in computer poetry*. Hanover, NH: University Press of New England.

Hayles, N. K. (2022) "Inside the mind of an AI: Materiality and the crisis of representation," *New Literary History*, 54(1), pp. 635–666. https://doi.org/10.1353/nlh.2022.a898324.

HeimrArnadalr (2018) "Ken M on Onomatopoeias," *r/KenM*. www.reddit.com/r/-KenM/comments/9du4rc/ken_m_on_onomatopoeias/ (Accessed: June 28, 2022).

Henrickson, L. (2021) "Constructing the other half of the policeman's beard." *Electronic Book Review*. https://doi.org/10.7273/2BT7-PW23.

Heras, D. C. (2019) "Spectacular machinery and encrypted spectatorship," *A Peer-Reviewed Journal About*, 8(1), pp. 170–182. https://doi.org/10.7146/aprja.v8i1.115423.

Hsu, J. (2014) "IBM's new brain," *IEEE Spectrum [News]*, 51(10), pp. 17–19. https://doi.org/10.1109/MSPEC.2014.6905473.

Irani, L. (2015) "The cultural work of microwork," *New Media & Society*, 17(5), pp. 720–739. https://doi.org/10.1177/1461444813511926.

Kang, M. (2011) *Sublime dreams of living machines: The automaton in the European imagination*. Cambridge, MA: Harvard University Press.

Keating, J. and Nourbakhsh, I. (2019) "Rossum's mimesis," in T. Heffernan (ed.) *Cyborg futures: Cross-disciplinary perspectives on artificial intelligence and robotics*. Cham: Springer (Social and cultural studies of robots and AI), pp. 141–158. https://doi.org/10.1007/978-3-030-21836-2.

Kirby, D. (2010) "The future is now: Diegetic prototypes and the role of popular films in generating real-world technological development," *Social Studies of Science*, 40(1), pp. 41–70. https://doi.org/10.1177/0306312709338325.

Kirschenbaum, M. (2023) *Prepare for the Textpocalypse*, *The Atlantic*. www.theatlantic.com/technology/archive/2023/03/ai-chatgpt-writing-language-models/673318/ (Accessed: June 7, 2023).

Knight, W. (2016) "Tougher Turing test exposes chatbots' stupidity," *MIT Technology Review*, 14 July. www.technologyreview.com/2016/07/14/7797/tougher-turing-test-exposes-chatbots-stupidity/ (Accessed: July 5, 2022).

Kubrick_Fan (2020) "This data is helpful, you should parse it as soon as possible," *r/totallynotrobots*. www.reddit.com/r/totallynotrobots/comments/jhblux/this_data_is_helpful_you_should_parse_it_as_soon/ (Accessed: January 20, 2021).

Laquintano, T. and Vee, A. (2017) "How automated writing systems affect the circulation of political information online." *Literacy in Composition Studies*, 5(2), pp. 43–62.

Lillywhite, A. (2018) "Is posthumanism a primitivism? Networks, fetishes, and race," *Diacritics*, 46(3), pp. 100–119. https://doi.org/10.1353/dia.2018.0018.

Live Eye Surveillance (no date). www.myliveeye.com/ (Accessed: July 9, 2022).

Mackenzie, A. (2015) "The production of prediction: What does machine learning want?" *European Journal of Cultural Studies*, 18(4–5), pp. 429–445. https://doi.org/10.1177/1367549415577384.

MacLeod, K. (2000) "The functions of the written text in practice-based PhD submissions," *Working Papers in Art and Design*, 1.

Mandelbaum, R. F. (2018) "Don't be fooled by the 'Forced a bot' meme," *Giƺmodo*, 14 June. https://gizmodo.com/dont-be-fooled-by-the-forced-a-bot-meme-1826832915 (Accessed: December 10, 2018).

Massumi, B. (2014) "Envisioning the virtual," in M. Grimshaw (ed.) *The Oxford handbook of virtuality*. Oxford: Oxford University Press, pp. 55–70.

McCarthy, L. (2017) *Lauren*. https://lauren-mccarthy.com (Accessed: July 9, 2022).

McCarthy, L. (2018) *Feeling at home: Between human and AI, medium*. https://immerse.news/feeling-at-home-between-human-and-ai-6047561e7f04 (Accessed: March 2, 2022).

Milner, R. M. (2016) *The world made meme: Public conversations and participatory media*. Cambridge: The MIT Press (The information society series).

Montfort, N., Baudoin, P., Bell, J., et al. (2013) *10 PRINT CHR$(205.5 +RND(1));:GOTO 10*. Cambridge, MA: MIT Press (Software studies).

Natale, S. (2021) *Deceitful media: Artificial intelligence and social life after the Turing test*. 1st ed. Oxford: Oxford University Press. https://doi.org/10.1093/oso/9780190080365.001.0001.

Ogden, B. (2010) "Benjamin, Wittgenstein, and philosophical anthropology: A reevaluation of the mimetic faculty," *Grey Room*, 39, pp. 57–73. https://doi.org/10.1162/grey.2010.1.39.57.

Parrish, A. (2021) *Language models can only write poetry, Decontextualiƺe*. https://posts.decontextualize.com/language-models-poetry (Accessed: December 14, 2021).

Pasquinelli, M. and Joler, V. (2020) *The Nooscope manifested: AI as instrument of knowledge extractivism*. https://nooscope.ai/.

Patti, K. (2018) *I forced a bot to watch over 1,000 hours of Olive Garden commercials and then asked it to write an Olive Garden commercial of its own*.

Here is the first page, Twitter. https://twitter.com/KeatonPatti/status/1006961202998726665 (Accessed: December 10, 2018).

Phillips, W. (2015) *This is why we can't have nice things: Mapping the relationship between online trolling and mainstream culture.* Cambridge, MA: The MIT Press (The information society series).

Portela, M. (2013) *Scripting reading motions: The codex and the computer as self-reflexive machines.* Cambridge: MIT Press.

Potolsky, M. (2006) *Mimesis.* New York: Routledge (The new critical idiom).

Rabinbach, A. (1979) "Introduction to Walter Benjamin's 'Doctrine of the Similar'," *New German Critique*, 17, pp. 60–64. https://doi.org/10.2307/488009.

Racter, Chamberlain, W. and Etter, T. (1984) *The policeman's beard is half constructed: Computer prose and poetry by Racter.* New York: Warner Books.

Replika (no date). https://replika.ai (Accessed: July 5, 2022).

Rettberg, S. (2019) *Electronic literature.* Cambridge: Polity Press.

Rettberg, S. (2023) "Cyborg authorship: Writing with AI – Part 1; The trouble(s) with ChatGPT," *Electronic Book Review.* https://doi.org/10.7273/5SY5-RX37.

Reydal (2016) "Welcome to totallynotrobots: Subreddit explanation and full rules here." *r/totallynotrobots.* www.reddit.com/r/totallynotrobots/comments/4ej36f/sticky_welcome_to_totallynotrobots_subreddit/ (Accessed: January 20, 2021).

r/totallynotrobots [Totally Not Robots] (no date) *Reddit.* www.reddit.com/r/totallynotrobots/ (Accessed: January 20, 2021).

RyanTheRyno (2016) "What if there was someone here who was a robot pretending to be a not robot?" *r/totallynotrobots.* https://np.reddit.com/r/totallynotrobots/comments/4g6q45/what_if_there_was_someone_here_who_was_a_robot/ (Accessed: January 20, 2021).

Saum-Pascual, A. (2020) "Is third generation literature postweb literature? And why should we care?" *Electronic Book Review*. https://doi.org/10.7273/60pg-1574.

Schaffer, S. (1999) "Enlightened automata," in W. Clark, J. Golinski, and S. Schaffer (eds.) *The sciences in enlightened Europe*. Chicago: University of Chicago Press, pp. 126–165.

Schwartz, O. (2018) "Competing visions for AI," *Digital Culture & Society*, 4(1), pp. 87–106. https://doi.org/10.14361/dcs-2018-0107.

Schwartz, O. and Laird, B. (no date) *Bot or not*. http://botpoet.com/ (Accessed: October 9, 2020).

Seaver, N. (2017) "Algorithms as culture: Some tactics for the ethnography of algorithmic systems," *Big Data & Society*, 4(2), p. 205395171773810. https://doi.org/10.1177/2053951717738104.

Simanowski, R. (2011) *Digital art and meaning: Reading kinetic poetry, text machines, mapping art, and interactive installations*. Minneapolis: University of Minnesota Press (Electronic Mediations, 35).

Spool, A. (2015) *Ken M, know your meme*. https://knowyourmeme.com/memes/ken-m (Accessed: June 28, 2022).

Stein, G. (2005) *Tender buttons: Objects – Food – Rooms*. Project Gutenberg. http://www.gutenberg.org/ebooks/15396.

Stengers, I. (2005) "The cosmopolitical proposal," in B. Latour and P. Weibel (eds.) *Making things public: Atmospheres of democracy*, Cambridge: The MIT Press, pp. 1–16.

Stengers, I. (2012) "Reclaiming animism," *E-flux journal*, 36 (7), pp. 1–9. www.e-flux.com/journal/36/61245/reclaiming-animism/.

Strachey, C. (1954) "The 'Thinking' machine," *Encounter*, 3(4), pp. 25–31.

Taussig, M. T. (1993) *Mimesis and alterity: A particular history of the senses*. New York: Routledge.

Torres, R. and Marques, D. (2020) "The cyberliterary efficacy of combinatory literature in urban cishet university students (or how to imagine a paper by programming an abstract)," *The Digital Review*. https://doi .org/10.7273/3vnt-my71.

Tubaro, P., Casilli, A. A. and Coville, M. (2020) "The trainer, the verifier, the imitator: Three ways in which human platform workers support artificial intelligence," *Big Data & Society*, 7(1), pp. 1–12. https://doi .org/10.1177/2053951720919776.

Turing, A. (2004) "Computing machinery and intelligence," in J. Copeland (ed.) *The essential turing: Seminal writings in computing, logic, philosophy, artificial intelligence, and artificial life plus The secrets of enigma*. Oxford: Clarendon Press, pp. 441–464.

Turkle, S. (2007) "Authenticity in the age of digital companions," *Interaction studies*, 8(3), pp. 501–517.

Unknown (no date) "File:ELIZA conversation.png," *Wikimedia Commons*. https://commons.wikimedia.org/wiki/File:ELIZA_conversation.png (Accessed: June 4, 2023).

Visti, A. (no date) *code&share//*.https://codeandshare.net/ (Accessed: January 20, 2021).

Visti, A. and Erslev, M. S. (2021) *Aarhus Urban Operating System* [Website]. https://aauos.online/ (Accessed: September 14, 2021).

Vogel, E. et al. (2021) "Thinking with imposters: The imposter as analytic," in E. Vogel et al. (eds.) *The imposter as social theory: Thinking with gatecrashers, cheats and charlatans*. Bristol: Bristol University Press, pp. 1–29.

von Kempelen, W. (1783) "Türkischen Schachspielers," *Wikimedia Commons*. https://commons.wikimedia.org/w/index.php?curid=424092 (Accessed: June 4, 2023).

Wardrip-Fruin, N. (2011) "Digital media archaeology," in J. Parikka and E. Huhtamo (eds.) *Media archaeology: Approaches, applications, and implications*. Berkeley, CA: University of Minnesota Press, pp. 302–322.

Weizenbaum, J. (1966) "ELIZA – A computer program for the study of natural language communication between man and machine," *Communications of the ACM*, 9(1), pp. 36–45. https://doi.org/10.1145/365153.365168.

Whalen, D. Z. (2021) "Computer-generated books: Metonymic, metaphoric and operationalist," in *ELO Conference and Media Festival 2021: Platform (Post?) Pandemic*. https://elmcip.net/critical-writing/gener ated-word-metonymic-generic-and-operationalist.

Wolin, R. (1982) "Benjamin's materialist theory of experience," *Theory and Society*, 11(1), pp. 17–42. https://doi.org/10.1007/BF00173108.

Acknowledgments

I would like to thank Anders Visti, Christian Hagelskjær From, Nathália Novais, Mace Ojala, Conrad Reuter, Paweł Gach, Winnie Soon, Gabriel Pereira, and Heidi Nikolaisen for participating in and enabling the practice-based research on the basis of which this Element exists. My sincere thanks to the anonymous reviewers, whose insightful criticism has been very helpful in whipping my argument into shape. Thanks to Søren Pold for generative discussions and valuable feedback. And to Lea, Kai, and Birk, to whom I dedicate this work.

Cambridge Elements ⹀

Publishing and Book Culture

SERIES EDITOR

Samantha Rayner
University College London

Samantha Rayner is Professor of Publishing and Book Cultures at UCL. She is also Director of UCL's Centre for Publishing, co-Director of the Bloomsbury CHAPTER (Communication History, Authorship, Publishing, Textual Editing and Reading) and co-Chair of the Bookselling Research Network.

ASSOCIATE EDITOR

Leah Tether
University of Bristol

Leah Tether is Professor of Medieval Literature and Publishing at the University of Bristol. With an academic background in medieval French and English literature and a professional background in trade publishing, Leah has combined her expertise and developed an international research profile in book and publishing history from manuscript to digital.

About the Series

This series aims to fill the demand for easily accessible, quality texts available for teaching and research in the diverse and dynamic fields of Publishing and Book Culture. Rigorously researched and peer-reviewed Elements will be published under themes, or 'Gatherings'. These Elements should be the first check point for researchers or students working on that area of publishing and book trade history and practice: we hope that, situated so logically at Cambridge University Press, where academic publishing in the UK began, it will develop to create an unrivalled space where these histories and practices can be investigated and preserved.

Cambridge Elements ☰

Publishing and Book Culture

Digital Literary Culture

Gathering Editor: Laura Dietz

Laura Dietz is Associate Professor of Writing and Digital
Publishing Studies in the Cambridge School of Creative
Industries at Anglia Ruskin University. She writes novels and
studies novels, publishing fiction alongside research on topics
such as e-novel readership, the digital short story, online
literary magazines, and the changing definition of authorship in
the digital era.

Printed in the United States
by Baker & Taylor Publisher Services